101 TOP HISTORICAL SITES OF
CUBA

ALSO BY ALAN TWIGG

First Invaders: The Literary Origins of British Columbia (2004)
Intensive Care: A Memoir (2002)
Cuba: A Concise History for Travellers (2000)
Twigg's Directory of 1001 B.C. Writers (1992)
Strong Voices: Conversations with 50 Canadian Authors (1988)
Vander Zalm: From Immigrant to Premier (1986)
Vancouver and Its Writers (1986)
Hubert Evans: The First Ninety-Three Years (1985)
For Openers: Conversations with 24 Canadian Writers (1981)

101 TOP HISTORICAL SITES OF
CUBA

ALAN TWIGG

PROSPECT BOOKS
VANCOUVER, BC

This book is published by Beach Holme Publishing, Suite 1010, 409 Granville Street, Vancouver, B.C. V6C 1T2. *www.beachholme.bc.ca*. This is a Prospect Book.

The publisher gratefully acknowledges the financial support of the Canada Council for the Arts and of the British Columbia Arts Council. The publisher also acknowledges the financial assistance received from the Government of Canada through the Book Publishing Industry Development Program (BPIDP) for its publishing activities.

The Canada Council | Le Conseil des Arts
for the Arts | du Canada

BRITISH
COLUMBIA
ARTS COUNCIL
Supported by the Province of British Columbia

Editor: Michael Carroll
Design and Production: Jen Hamilton
Cover Art: Copyright © 2004 by Alan Twigg

Printed and bound in Canada by AGMV Marquis Imprimeur

Library and Archives Canada Cataloguing in Publication Data

Twigg, Alan, 1952–
    101 top historical sites of Cuba/by Alan Twigg.

"A Prospect book."
ISBN 0-88878-440-6

    1. Historic sites—Cuba—Guidebooks. 2. Cuba—Guidebooks.
I. Title. II. Title: One hundred and one top historical sites of Cuba.

F1759.7.T84 2004   917.29104'64   C2003-910070-7

To L. in Guantánamo, to J. and his lovely family
in Santiago de Cuba, to E. in Santiago, and to the many other
Cubans I will not forget—with added thanks to everyone at
Hostal Valencia in Havana, where much of this text was written.

CONTENTS

INTRODUCTION
CHEZ FIDEL

People ask: What do you remember most? What shouldn't I miss? It's impossible to say. So much depends on who you were with at the time. Or the troubles you took to get someplace.

A spontaneous swim by the side of the road. A chicken dinner in someone's house. The misunderstandings, the many kindnesses. The strange twists of fate. The fleeting grins of kids as you wave. We travel to get lost and found again. If you're a photographer, you remember the way the light falls. If you're a musician, you remember the clicking of heels.

Everybody collects their own precious memories and you needn't hear about mine. The only exception I'll make is for the one site you probably won't be able to see—Fidel Castro's off-limits birthplace in Birán.

Having written a history of Cuba, I was determined to see where Castro grew up. He is such a fascinating and contradictory character that the clues to his megalomania could only be found in the past, when he was still in his formative stages, before the whole world was his stage.

That's why I hired a private car in Guantánamo. It was the only way I could get to the remote homestead in Holguín Province where Castro was born. My driver was a hustler in his mid-twenties named Orlando. Whenever we went down a long hill, he turned off the engine of his vintage Pontiac to save gas. We both knew that renting his family's patched-together vehicle was illegal, but we also both knew that discussing it was next to pointless.

Like most Cubans, Orlando was well educated. He knew

I hadn't come to Cuba for girls or cigars. I explained what I was up to. I told him that as a Canadian I hoped I had a fairly neutral perspective—somewhere between the narrow views of the American government and the vainglorious posturings of Fidel. I told him my history of Cuba was far more critical of the Americans than Fidel, but Cuban authorities probably wouldn't bother to see it that way; they'd flip straight to the Dictatorship Index, or the parts of Fidel's love life, and that's all they would see.

He nodded. Born after the revolution, without any memories of the dictator Fulgencio Batista, or of the American Mafia that ran the brothels and casinos and turned Havana into a cheap Babylon, Orlando wasn't cynical about Cuba, only realistic. He was willing to express some reservations about Cuban society, but he dare not say anything critical about Castro the man.

It was late afternoon when we arrived at the remote hacienda called Manacas near Birán. The sky was dark with clouds, and it was starting to rain. There was a chain stretched across the dirt road, about a half metre high. Underneath some trees, to the right, was a semi-derelict shack with a porch where two unshaven soldiers were biding their time. The house where Castro was born and raised was less than 100 metres away.

I slipped my miniature Olympus into the pocket of my pants before I got out of the old Pontiac. A tense, diplomatic confrontation ensued. The older guard, the more sullen of the two, did all the talking. He explained in no uncertain terms that visitors were simply not allowed on the site. I didn't have to wait for Orlando's translation.

It began to rain much harder. I asked Orlando to ask the guards if we might take shelter under their porch. Entrusted with the tedious job of preventing access to one of the most private places on El Presidente's island, these two guys weren't in any position to afford civility, but there seemed to be no harm in letting us stand out of the downpour.

I had to get a picture. While writing about Cuba I had become intrigued by tales of the very odd Castro family that seldom ate together. According to one biographer, that's why Fidel Castro became accustomed to eating many of his meals standing up. Castro's older half brother, Pedro Emilio, had portrayed the family's lack of harmony in a radio soap opera called *The Castros of Birán* until he was persuaded—likely with money from his father—to discontinue the series.

Fidel Alejandro Castro Ruz was born out of wedlock during a cyclone on August 13, 1926, at approximately 2:00 a.m. Having been born in 1926, he would attack the Moncada Army Barracks at age 26 on July 26, giving rise to his July 26 Movement that martyred his co-revolutionary Frank País, the other formative leader in Cuba's revolution.

The Castros' wooden house was on stilts in the Galician style. Castro's father was a Gallego from the northern province of Galicia in Spain. He'd fought for Spain on the losing side of the so-called Spanish-American War. That war was chiefly fought between the Cubans and Spain until an opportunistic United States of America joined the indigenous rebels in the closing stages. An easy victory at San Juan Hill in 1898 later vaulted Theodore Roosevelt into the American vice presidency due to trumped-up reportage in the jingoistic U.S. press from the likes of a rookie reporter named Winston Churchill.

Leonard Wood, an American general, governed Cuba at the start of the 20th century. He wrote to President William McKinley: "The people here...know they aren't ready for self-government. We are dealing with a race which has been steadily going down for a hundred years and into which we have got to infuse new life, new principles, and new methods of doing things." The Americans granted themselves a lease on their new Guantánamo Bay Naval Base in perpetuity in 1903, the same year the United Fruit Company purchased 200,000 coastal acres for $400,000. By 1905 approximately one-quarter of Cuba was owned by Americans.

After a brief postwar return to Spain, Angel Castro came back to Cuba and worked as a day labourer for the United Fruit Company in eastern Cuba. He became a sugarcane contractor and eventually a wealthy landowner, marrying a respectable schoolteacher. She bore him two children, but this marriage unravelled when Castro Senior turned his attentions to an illiterate, teenage housemaid named Lina Ruz González—Fidel Castro's mother—who, legend has it, had travelled the length of Cuba in an oxcart with her father from Pinar del Río Province in the west.

When Castro was a boy, farm animals had taken shelter underneath the house. Everything was preserved as it was. From the porch, peering through the rain, I could see a few horses with free run of the place. Here Castro had developed his particular interest in animal husbandry. The homestead at Birán had hosted a slaughterhouse, a rudimentary school, a store, a bakery, and a post office. "Everyone lavished attention on me, flattered and treated me differently from the other boys we played with when we were children," he once recalled. "These other children went barefoot while we wore shoes."

With my inadequate Spanish, it was easy to appear feckless. The guards were willing to wait us out until I got bored. Body language is universal. I was just one more

4

naive gringo prepared to view Cuba as a tourist paradise. I tried to give no indication that I had been interrogated in a windowless concrete room for more than half an hour because I was carrying books about Cuba that *might* contain some criticism of Castro's regime.

One of the four books confiscated from me at the airport—one entering the country and three leaving it—had included the English text of Che Guevara's own speeches, a book I'd purchased from a government bookstand in Cuba on a preceding visit *before* my history of Cuba had been published by Penguin Books. I was well aware of the stringent repression of intellectuals and knew enough about Cuban jails from Amnesty International reports to know they had provided some of the most unforgiving conditions on the planet.

Of the hundred or so books I've read about Cuba, some of the most illuminating were the works of Guillermo Cabrera Infante, the brilliant dissident, and Jon Lee Anderson's superb biography *Che Guevara: A Revolutionary Life*. The comment from Castro's estranged daughter, Alina Fernández—"My father's island is nothing but an enormous prison"—doesn't represent the whole truth about the country and its superb people, but dismissing her condemnation as unfounded is equally invalid. The citizens of Cuba are not free to leave. Many continually risk their lives, and die, attempting to escape.

We were allowed to stay under the porch because of the downpour. I had Orlando make unwelcome chitchat with the head guard for about 15 minutes, hoping the guards would recognize we didn't pose any threat. But it was clear they weren't even comfortable with us *looking* toward the homestead, let alone taking pictures. It wasn't exactly the Cuban Missile Crisis, but clearly we were locked into opposing camps, playing a weird waiting game.

The building had no amenities, no electricity, no heat. The surrounding farmland was deserted for kilometres. A guy could take a leak anywhere. I asked if there was a washroom. They nodded toward the interior of the dank guard station. Inside I found the remnants of some indoor plumbing—a toilet without water. The porcelain bowl wasn't filthy so much as it was black. I tried not to use my imagination. The guardhouse had rectangular openings in the walls for ventilation, without glass. As soon as I was away from the guards, I went a few feet down a little hallway and found an unobstructed viewpoint of the house.

Darkness was descending. It was pouring. I only had a pint-size camera. Without a zoom I knew I wasn't going to get much. I leaned around an open sill, taking a second to steady myself. It was a documentary impulse. I didn't realize I'd ever be making a book about historical sites. I wanted to understand the circumstances that gave rise to Fidel Castro. I knew that in the early 1900s Castro's father had functioned like the local czar, a feudal landlord. His word was law. It seemed logical, even obvious, that Castro's model for power was his father. The son had grown up and administered his island much as the father had administered his remote holdings in Oriente (now Holguín) Province.

The crude homestead was a large chunk of Cuban history and psychological territory. Both Castro's mother and father had modest graves nearby. Possibly Castro was planning on being buried here. Manacas is a shrine Castro has reserved for himself. It's hallowed ground, part of a radically private life. Castro's homestead is even more difficult to visit on an official basis than his beloved mountain, Pico Turquino. A man who is prone to making eight-hour speeches, Castro claims he doesn't want to encourage hero worship or draw too much attention to himself.

For such a strongman, a classic *caudillo*, it's known that Castro can be extraordinarily vain. As his former friend Gabriel García Márquez put it, "I do not think anyone in the world could be a worse loser." Castro is sensitive about his personal, as opposed to political, reputation to an extreme. There is much in Castro's past that has been kept under wraps, such as his sexual relationships and the identities of his nine (known) children via five women.

The flash went off. I cursed the blackening sky and my amateurism. Having published hundreds of photographs over the years, I retained the foolhardy notion that all one needs to be a half-ass photographer is a practised eye, lots of film, and a decent camera. I hastily took two more shots, frightened that the flashes or the clicks of the Olympus would be noticeable from the front porch, only about five metres away from where I stood at the side of the building.

Castro's rough childhood gave rise to his brazen machismo. It's well documented that Castro was a gun-toting hoodlum back in the days when he and his younger brother, Raúl, attended university in Havana. Murders of rival gang members weren't uncommon. Homosexuals and dissidents have received brutal treatment from Castro's regime during his 45 years in unelected office. Only North Korea's dictator Kim Il Sung has been in power longer than Castro. I believe knowledge of the environs where such an extraordinary person was raised should be in the public domain. That's why I took the fuzzy photo through the rain.

In retrospect, it was a very dumb thing to do. When we got safely back to the Pontiac, Orlando told me he had seen three flashes of light over the shoulder of the main guard. If you're a photographer, you remember the light.

7

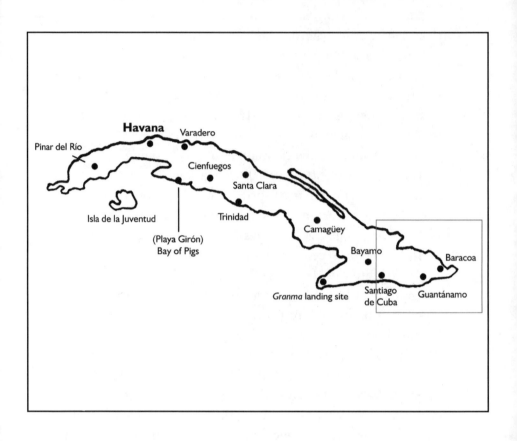

Fidel Castro's rebels shared this one guitar and later signed it.

Havana is the economic centre, Varadero is the focal point for tourism, but Cuba's revolutionary spirit arose from the eastern end of the island. To serve history this book starts at Baracoa, the second-oldest European settlement in the Americas (after Santo Domingo). It's an exotic, peaceful, and remote town accessible by the magnificent and sometimes harrowing (at night) La Farola Highway over the mountains from Guantánamo. Direct flights are also available from Havana. Nearby Santiago de Cuba is the country's second-largest city and mustn't be missed. Here Fidel Castro began his revolutionary movement in 1953 by attacking the Moncada Army Barracks.

The church custodian *(right)* in Baracoa poses with the author and the Cross of Parra, aka the Cross of Columbus, supposedly erected in 1492.

I. CROSS OF PARRA

Catedral de Nuestra Señora de la Asunción, Parque Central, Baracoa

In this ramshackle church built in 1833 you'll find a wooden cross said to be the oldest European-made relic in the Americas. This cross serves as an irresistible starting point for a tour of Cuba, whether you believe it's real or not. According to the church custodian, the Cross of Parra was erected by Christopher Columbus in 1492, one of 29 crosses left on his first voyage. It's made of uvilla wood but was placed near a parra tree, hence the name. It's now protected in a glass case near the altar because local fishermen were taking chips as talismans, eroding its size over the centuries. Skeptics will say if you believe that one, you might be interested in buying the Brooklyn Bridge. Cuba's first tourist didn't have a priest aboard for his historic first voyage, but we know from Columbus's diary that he did leave a cross at Baracoa on December 1, 1492. After Fidel Castro's revolution in 1959, the Cross of Parra became a symbol of colonialism and lost much of its appeal. Even today there is no signage, minimal security for it, and no admission fee to see it. To resurrect its reputation, Baracoa's chief historian, Dr. Alejandro Hartmann Matos, initiated carbon-14 testing by the Universidad Católica de Lobaina La Nueva in Brussels in 1988. Belgian scientist Dr. Roger Dechamps, a wood expert and author of more than 50 books, determined the wood was from the Caribbean, not Spain. Hartmann and Deschamps published their research in European scientific and popular journals in the early 1990s. The carbon-14 tests supported the claim that wood in the Cross of Parra was growing prior to 1492.

El Yunque is the "squarish mountain" that Christopher Columbus described when he moored in Cuba in what is now called Bahía de Baracoa.

2. EL YUNQUE

Mountaintop, south of Baracoa

Having seen Cuba for the first time on October 27, 1492, Christopher Columbus declared it was the most beautiful island he had ever seen. He anchored at Baracoa with two of his three ships, *Nina* and *Santa Maria*, on November 27, 1492. During that first visit, Columbus described "a squarish mountain that looks like an island." This distinctive tabletop mountain is El Yunque de Baracoa, meaning "solid like a fort." Often described as an anvil, El Yunque is the strongest evidence that Columbus moored here for one week, his longest moorage in the Caribbean. The best view of El Yunque is from the Hotel El Castillo swimming pool atop the hill. Tourists who want to sleep nearest to where Columbus might have stepped ashore can stay at the up-market but dull Hotel Porto Santo, near the airport. Again there is no signage. Approximately 150 kilometres to the northwest, the town of Gibara, with a similar mountain, claims to be the site of Columbus's first visit.

3. MUSEO MUNICIPAL (BARACOA)
Calle José Martí near the Malecón

Baracoa was established when Diego Velázquez de Cuéllar arrived with 300 men in 1511. Below ground level, down a few steps, outside, you can see the original Spanish foundations of the second-oldest town in the New World. It served as the first capital of Cuba until it was eclipsed by Santiago de Cuba in 1515. An anthropological exhibit also pays tribute to the Taínos, an agricultural people said to have migrated from present-day Venezuela. A yearlong expedition in 1988 proved this migration was feasible in dugout canoes. The museum has hosted annual Taíno conferences since 1997. It also provides background about an infamous character named El Pelú, an unkempt and unwelcome

Dr. Alejandro Hartmann Matos *(far right)*, the curator at Baracoa's Museo Municipal, poses with some fellow Baracoans.

vagabond who cursed the townspeople and fled into the mountains at the end of the 19th century. His curse, known as *la maldición del Pelú*, reputedly helped keep Baracoans in extreme isolation and illiteracy until Fidel Castro vanquished El Pelú's curse in 1960. Baracoa was nonetheless the last town in Cuba to achieve widespread public literacy.

4. BUST OF HATUEY, FIRST MARTYR FOR FREEDOM

Parque Central, Baracoa

Hatuey, Cuba's first revolutionary martyr, was burned at the stake in 1512.

Burned alive by the Spanish for organizing resistance in 1512, Hatuey is celebrated throughout the country as Cuba's first "internationalist," the forerunner of Argentina's Che Guevara. A Taíno chieftain who had fled Hispaniola, Hatuey warned Indians in Baracoa about the brutality of the Spaniards and led the first Cuban resistance against foreign control during the early 1500s at Baracoa. In 1953 sculptor Rita Longa provided Baracoa with her famous bust of the defiant Hatuey accusingly facing the town's main church—an image revised for the label of Hatuey beer. Before he was burned alive at the stake, Hatuey asked if there would be Spaniards in heaven. When a priest told him yes, Hatuey declared he preferred to go to hell.

5. GUAMÁ'S LAND

Boca de Yumurí, 15 minutes east of Baracoa by car

The local Baracoa chief named Guamá refused to surrender to the Spanish after Hatuey was killed in 1512. Instead Guamá laid siege to Baracoa and Puerto Principe, setting fire to the Spanish outposts and qualifying as Cuba's first homegrown resistance leader. By the time the Spanish were able to locate Guamá's whereabouts in 1532, he had died of natural causes. Within a hundred years of European contact, the indigenous people of Cuba were virtually

Descendants of Guamá, Cuba's first indigenous freedom fighter, can still be found In Boca de Yumurí near the mouth of Río Yumurí.

extinct. Centuries later residents of a nearby hamlet called Cañon del Río Yumurí, approximately 30 kilometres southeast of Baracoa, are the only Cubans assumed to exhibit "original" Indian features and customs. Sculptor Ramón Dominguez's statue honouring Guamá can be found on Calle Coroneles Galano in Baracoa; Boca de Yumurí is within easy walking distance of the mouth of Río Yumurí.

6. HOTEL LA RUSA
Waterfront at Calle Máximo Gómez No. 161, Baracoa

When visiting Baracoa, most well-to-do tourists prefer to stay at Hotel El Castillo on Calle Calixto García, converted from the Castillo Santa Barbara, but Hotel La Rusa has a more colourful history. Baracoa's first modern 12-room hotel was established by Magdalena Menase, a Russian aristocrat and amateur Parisian opera singer who fled the Russian Revolution with her husband and came to Baracoa in 1929. Magdalena arrived at a time when Baracoa was exporting four to five million bananas to the United States annually. She and her husband first built a shop, then started their hotel on the Malecón in 1953. After her husband died and Errol Flynn was a guest, both in 1956, La Rusa became one of Fidel Castro's most important supporters. She gave $25,000 in 1959 to buy arms and planes. After Fidel, Raúl Castro, and Che Guevara were her hotel guests on January 29, 1960, the revolutionary government demonstrated its appreciation for her help by beginning work on La Farola, the magnificent highway that finally connected Baracoa to the rest of Cuba in 1964. Cuban politicians had continually promised to complete a public highway to Baracoa and never delivered. Magdalena was active in the

Hotel La Rusa, once owned by Russian opera singer Magdalena Menase, was visited by Fidel and Raúl Castro and Che Guevara in 1960 as a thank-you to the hotelier who donated $25,000 to the revolution.

Federation of Cuban Women and the Cuban Red Cross, and is immortalized as the character of Vera in *La Consagración de la Primavera* (*The Consecration of Spring*) by Alejo Carpentier, who mainly lived in Paris but visited Baracoa in 1968. La Rusa died on September 5, 1978, at an undetermined age.

7. RÍO DE MIEL (HONEY RIVER)
Ensenada de Miel, Baracoa

There is no honey at the Honey River, but a legend has been cultivated: in the early 1800s a young Frenchwoman, Danilla, was in love with a Baracoan Indian, Alejandro. The French in Baracoa were supposed to leave for the United States in the morning, due to the Napoleonic Wars, so the unwed couple went to the Río de Miel and made love all night.

When Cuba's Spanish conqueror, Diego Velázquez, married Juana de Cuéllar in Baracoa in 1512, he became the first Christian groom in the Americas.

Danilla stayed. People now say that anyone who bathes in the Río de Miel will either return to Baracoa or remain in Baracoa. It's one of the earliest tales of interracial romantic love in Cuba. More historic is the 1512 union in Baracoa between Diego Velázquez and Juana de Cuéllar, daughter of a Santo Domingo administrator. The high-society bride died only one week later. Theirs was the first Christian marriage to be consecrated in the Americas.

This painting depicts the death of freedom fighter Antonio Maceo in 1896.

8. MONUMENTO A ANTONIO MACEO (BARACOA)

One kilometre west of Baracoa, beside the airport runway

Due to its remoteness, Baracoa was chosen for a rendezvous of insurrectionists José Martí, Antonio Maceo, Maximo Gómez, Calixto García, Limbano Sánchez, and Sánchez Echeverría in April 1895. Maceo came from Costa Rica via Jamaica and Santo Domingo and ultimately liberated Baracoa. An annual party on this otherwise deserted spot marks Baracoa's status as one of Cuba's first independent towns. Approachable by a bumpy dirt track, this Maceo statue marks the birthplace of the movement that led to the overthrow of the Spanish in 1898. The statue honours the mulatto general as the "personification of protest and heroism," someone with "the arm of Hercules and the tempest of a horse." He died of battle wounds in western Cuba on December 7, 1896.

The peninsular location this memorial provides is the best view for El Yunque as Christopher Columbus must have seen it from his ship.

9. GUANTÁNAMO U.S. NAVAL BASE

Between Baracoa and Santiago de Cuba, 21 kilometres south of Guantánamo

In 1903, in keeping with the Platt Amendment imposed by the United States, Cuba lost 116 square kilometres in perpetuity for the Guantánamo Naval Base. This base was primarily intended to safeguard shipping interests for the Panama Canal. In 1934 the United States under President Franklin Roosevelt modified the original "agreement" to a 99-year lease.

This 19th-century cartoon shows Uncle Sam stomping on the island of Cuba. In the 21st century the United States has used its naval base at Guantánamo—the oldest U.S. military installation on foreign soil—for interrogation of suspected terrorists outside international law.

Castro has long refused to cash the annual $4,000 lease payment sent each year by the United States and has repeatedly said the military base should be converted to a hospital to serve all the Caribbean. In 2002 the base was transformed into a prison for alleged Al-Qaeda terrorists and Taliban fighters. Some 400 Filipinos were hired to construct maximum-security cells at the Radio Range area of the base. Sensory-deprivation techniques used on the "detainees" caused international alarm.

The base has always been strictly off-limits for everyone except a few Cubans who can perform menial jobs. For a long time the installation was the most luxurious neighbourhood in Cuba, home to 7,000 people, with a golf course, McDonald's, and five movie theatres. The base is scheduled to revert to Cuban sovereignty in 2033. With 24-hour notice it's possible to gain access to an otherwise off-limits Cuban hilltop for a view of the oldest U.S. military base on foreign soil. Also there's a viewpoint south of Guantánamo at Caimanera.

10. CEMENTERIO SANTA IFIGENIA

Santiago de Cuba, off Avenida Crombet, one kilometre northwest of the Bacardi Rum Factory

Here is a flag-draped casket for José Martí, the most widely admired Cuban patriot and poet. Martí's tomb is the most revered place in the country, with the possible exception of the Virgin of Copper Basilica in Cobre and Che Guevara's tomb in Santa Clara. The hexagonal mausoleum was built in 1951, with each side representing one of the six original provinces of Cuba. The tomb of Carlos Manuel

Poet and patriot José Martí's tomb in Cementario Santa Ifigenia is a place of pilgrimage for those who revere the memory of one of the founding fathers of Cuban independence.

de Céspedes, "Father of the Fatherland," the most important nationalist hero prior to José Martí, is also here. Scattered throughout the grounds are graves for Cuba's first president, Tomás Estrada Palma, as well as the plots for the widow of Antonio Maceo; his much-revered mother, Mariana Grajales; and the País brothers, Frank and Josue. The gateway commemorates the Cuban soldiers who died in Angola; red-and-black flags mark the graves of those who fought with Castro at the Moncada Army Barracks.

II. BACARDÍ RUM FACTORY
Santiago de Cuba, Avenida Jesús Menédez near Calle Narciso López

Emilio Bacardí y Moreau (1844–1922) was the first mayor of Santiago de Cuba after the Spanish were ousted. The Bacardí family established their Santiago Caney Rum Distillery here in 1838 but took its patent with them to Puerto Rico after the Cuban revolution, renaming their product Bacardí rum. Still operational, this distillery welcomes tourists but makes little connection to its capitalist roots. The Bacardí home has been converted into a restaurant at Calle Bartolomé Masó No. 354 between Calles Pio Rosado and Hartmann. In 1899 Emilio Bacardí y Moreau founded Santiago de Cuba's oldest museum on Pio Rosada, between Calles Heredia and Aguilera. Upstairs is the impressive and fanciful depiction of Father Bartolomé de Las Casas, the protector of the Indians, discussing Cuban society with Hernán Cortéz. It's an unforgettable image for anyone who has even a slight understanding of the genocide that ensued. The Taíno people hover to the left of their would-be saviour Las Casas. Unfortunately the Bacardí Museum won't allow photos to be taken of the paintings by the Tejada brothers.

Rum baron Emilio Bacardí y Moreau's tomb can be found in Cementario Santa Ifigenia in Santiago de Cuba.

12. MUSEO-CASA NATAL DE ANTONIO MACEO

Santiago de Cuba, Calle Los Maceos No. 207 at Calle Mariano Corona

Antonio Maceo (1845–1896) grew up here, but he was actually born in Majaguabo in Santiago de Cuba Province. A black man and a freemason, he fought in two wars for independence and is renowned as the Bronze Titan.

Seen here as a young man, Antonio Maceo would later be known as the Bronze Titan for his heroic efforts in Cuba's struggle to win its independence from Spain in the 1890s.

24

13. CASA MUSEO DE FRANK Y JOSUE PAÍS

Santiago de Cuba, Calle General Banderas No. 226

The País brothers are two of the reasons why Santiago de Cuba is the island's official Hero City of the Republic of Cuba. Frank País was the most important revolutionary leader during the uprising in Santiago de Cuba that accompanied Fidel Castro's landing. He was killed by Fulgencio Batista's police on July 30, 1957; his brother, Josue, didn't last much longer. Whereas Castro cultivated the revolutionary limelight, the young Baptist schoolteacher Frank País was a self-sacrificing hero who organized and fought from within the belly of the beast.

Frank País, seen here in a picture adorning his gravestone, was a Baptist schoolteacher who led the insurrection that coincided with Fidel Castro's invasion of Cuba.

There is another museum, Museo de la Lucha Clandestina, that commemorates the underground activities of País and his supporters. It can be found at Calle General Jesús Rabí No. 1 on the edge of the Tivoli district.

14. TOWN HALL (SANTIAGO DE CUBA)

Parque Céspedes, between Calles Felix Peña and General Lacret

Many central squares in Cuba are named for Carlos Manuel de Céspedes, who declared Cuban independence in 1869, but only this one can claim to be the birthplace of Fidel Castro's regime. Castro delivered a celebrated victory speech in Havana

British author Graham Greene wrote part of his novel *Our Man in Havana* in Hotel Casa Granda on Parque Céspedes near the town hall in Santiago de Cuba.

on January 8, 1959, as recorded by many historic photos, but El Jefe's first public ascension to power occurred here on the north side of Parque Céspedes at the centre of Santiago de Cuba when he appeared on the balcony of this town hall (Ayuntamiento) on January 1, 1959, to declare victory. Reopened in 1995, Hotel Casa Granda on the east side of this square was the setting for a scene in Graham Greene's novel *Our Man in Havana*. Greene's famous fiction portrays Cuba's degenerate gambling and prostitution culture and is not widely circulated in Cuba.

15. CASA DE DIEGO VELÁZQUEZ

Santiago de Cuba, Parque Céspedes, at Calle Felix Peña No. 602

Here, dating back to 1522, are the remains of the oldest European residence in the Americas. Diego Velázquez hid colonial gold in this house in an underground vault, now exposed for tourists, until it could be loaded on ships bound for Spain. As an administrator, Velázquez was less ruthless than many of his contemporaries. He founded most of Cuba's major town sites and is supposedly buried somewhere beneath the nearby cathedral. His restored home has examples of period furniture and some original brickwork. Nearby at Velázquez Balcony (corner of Calles

Spanish colonial gold was once kept in this underground vault in Casa de Diego Velázquez, the oldest house in the Americas.

Bartolomé Masó and Mariano Corono), you're permitted one panoramic photo of the harbour for one American dollar. You can see where the Spanish fleet was trapped inside Santiago de Cuba's historic harbour by the U.S. fleet in 1898. The Americans won a one-sided naval victory beyond the harbour on July 3, 1898, effectively ending the so-called Spanish–American War. Castillo El Morro provides an even better vantage point for imagining the futile attempts by the Spanish ships to escape the American blockade.

16. CATEDRAL DE NUESTRA SEÑORA DE LA ASUNCIÓN
Santiago de Cuba, south side of Parque Céspedes

Catholicism arrived with a vengeance in the 1500s when proliferation of the Roman Catholic faith was required in

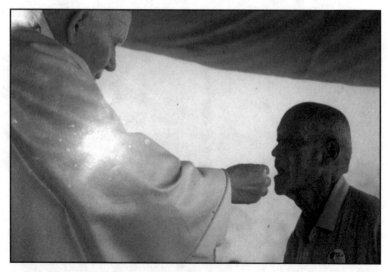

In 1998 Pope John Paul II gives his blessing to the Cuban caretaker from Catedral de Nuestra Señora de la Asunción in Baracoa.

return for territorial rights conferred by the pope. Cuba's first cathedral was built on this site in the 1520s. The current version dates from 1802. Other significant churches in Santiago de Cuba include Iglesia de Nuestra Señora de los Dolores, Iglesia de la Santísima Trinidad, Iglesia de Santo Tomás, and Iglesia de San Francisco, all from the 18th century. The Church served the aristocracy and did precious little to limit the cruelties and degradations of slavery. Hence when Fidel Castro took control of Cuba, the influence of Catholicism was deliberately emasculated until Pope John Paul II visited the country in 1998. El Papa celebrated Mass in Santiago de Cuba, blessing the Baracoan keeper of the Cross of Parra.

17. JOSÉ MARÍA DE HEREDIA BIRTHPLACE
Santiago de Cuba, Calle Heredia No. 260

Forced to live in exile because of his radical political beliefs, Cuba's leading 19th-century romantic poet, José María de Heredia (1803–1839), was the forerunner of more famous Cuban exiles such as José Martí and Fidel Castro. An extract of Heredia's most renowned work, *Ode to Niagara*, appears on the wall outside his home. Nearby at No. 208 is the former home of composer Rafael Salcedo (1844–1917), now renowned as the Casa de la Trova, where guitarists and troubadours perform. Many Cuban artists, in the tradition of Heredia, are still forced to live in exile, such as the brilliant satirist Guillermo Cabrera Infante, author of *Mea Cuba*.

An extract of poet José María de Heredia's most important work, *Ode to Niagara*, is affixed to the front of his birthplace in Santiago de Cuba.

18. MONCADA ARMY BARRACKS

Santiago de Cuba, off Avenida de los Libertadores, at Calle General Portuondo and Avenida Moncada

Fidel Castro's foolhardy attack at Gate Three of these barracks on July 26, 1953, gave rise to the name of his July 26 Movement and marked the beginning of his revolution. Now a school with a museum, the site is named for Cuban patriot Guillermón Moncada, imprisoned here by Spanish authorities in 1874. The current buildings were mostly constructed in 1938. Fulgencio Batista's army removed the bullet holes after Castro's inept attack; these have been "replaced" on the outer wall for dramatic effect. Within the extensive exhibit are photos of Castro touring this museum with the likes of Yasser

Now a school, the Moncada Army Barracks in Santiago de Cuba was the scene of Fidel Castro's failed 1953 attack.

Arafat. There is also a seldom-seen photo of Castro's lover and secretary Celia Sánchez with Raúl and Fidel Castro at their Sierra Maestra headquarters. Only Fidel the propagandist would have the genius to turn such a disastrous military defeat into a proud moment in Cuban history.

19. PARQUE HISTÓRICO ABEL SANTAMARÍA

Santiago de Cuba, west side of Avenida de los Libertadores, across from Museo Moncada

During the attack on the barracks, Abel Santamaría was sent by Fidel Castro to occupy a hospital on this site (since demolished) with his sister Haydée Santamaría and Melba Hernández. He was captured, tortured, and murdered. The viciousness of Fulgencio Batista's reprisals on the captured men stirred public opinion in favour of the rebels; Castro later immortalized the sacrifices of Abel Santamaría and his comrades in his famous defence address, *History Will*

Abel Santamaría *(centre with glasses)* is depicted with other *moncadistas* who were killed in the ill-fated assault on the Moncada Army Barracks on July 26, 1953.

Absolve Me, which he delivered at this location on October 16, 1953. Here, as well, Castro was tried and sentenced to prison on the Isla de Pinos (now called Isla de la Juventud). In prison Castro's men held educational sessions in the "Abel Santamaría Ideological Academy" in honour of their fallen colleague. The faces of Santamaría and José Martí share the monument in this park with the inscription DIED SO THE NATION COULD LIVE.

20. PALACIO DE JUSTICIA
Santiago de Cuba, Avenida de los Libertadores and Calle H

During the Moncada Army Barracks attack, a contingent led by Raúl Castro was supposed to provide covering fire from a rooftop at this site. The captured insurrectionists were tried and found guilty here in September 1953. The July 26 Movement survivors were defended at the Palacio de Justicia by Manuel Urrutia, the man Castro later named as the first Cuban president of his revolutionary regime on January 5, 1959. (Castro didn't make himself prime minister until February 16; he replaced Urrutia after Urrutia had resigned to protest Castro's sweeping agrarian reforms.) The Palacio de Justicia

From the roof of the Palacio de Justicia, Raúl Castro and a contingent of revolutionaries provided cover fire for his brother Fidel's attack on the Moncada Army Barracks.

is one more reminder that Raúl Castro has been subservient to his more dynamic older brother all his life. "I don't know how much he has been harmed by being my brother," says Fidel, "because, when there is a tall tree, it always casts a little shade on the others."

Near this "peace tree," Spain officially surrendered to the United States on August 12, 1898, ending the so-called Spanish-American War.

21. PEACE TREE
Santiago de Cuba, Avenida Raúl Pujol, east of Parque Zoológico

Here, under a huge ceiba tree, the Spanish garrison sur-rendered to American forces on August 12, 1898, ending four centuries of European control. In the process Cuba switched from Spanish to American masters. Today the remains of this Peace Tree are surrounded by a few old can-nons, seldom seen. The surrender of the Spanish occurred two weeks after the battle of San Juan Hill; the victorious but mostly black Cuban soldiers under General Calixto García weren't allowed to attend the surrender ceremony or even enter the city.

22. SAN JUAN HILL
Santiago de Cuba, east on Avenida Victoriano Garzón, then up Avenida Raúl Pujol

Theodore Roosevelt and his Rough Riders were glorified by the jingoist American presses of William Randolph Hearst and Joseph Pulitzer for their victorious battle here on July 1, 1898, but the outcome was a foregone conclusion. Outmanned and outgunned, the Spanish couldn't compete. One of the many plaques among the statuary here lists the American dead at less than 20 men. Just as John F. Kennedy's World War II wartime experiences were exag-gerated by his father for propaganda purposes to qualify him as presidential material, Teddy Roosevelt's reputation was "made" at San Juan Hill. Approximately 700 Spanish defenders on San Juan Hill held their ground all day long against 6,000 American troops.

A plaque commemorates Teddy Roosevelt and his Rough Riders' battle at San Juan Hill in Santiago de Cuba on July 1, 1898.

23. BOSQUE DE LOS MÁRTIRES DE BOLIVIA

Santiago de Cuba, Avenida de las Américas, bordered by Calles M and Terraza

This mound of earth looks more like a well-disguised underground bomb shelter than a memorial to great revolutionary heroes. Unmarked and unvisited, and rarely mentioned in guidebooks, this eerie site is ironically located almost kitty-corner to Hotel Santiago de Cuba, an ugly attempt to erect a swanky hotel for the Fourth Congress of the Communist Party of Cuba in 1991. It commemorates some of those who doggedly followed Che Guevara during his doomed Bolivian campaign, including the beautiful Haydée Tamara Bunke Bider, otherwise known as Tania. Painstakingly subtle images of Guevara and Tania aren't eye-catching unless you're standing three metres away from them. It's nonetheless a stirring place because it pays direct tribute to Guevara's East German lover, Tania, a mysterious woman more revered abroad than even Celia Sánchez. Possibly a double agent, Tania the Guerrilla wrote romantic poetry and was killed by Bolivian soldiers in 1967. Her official profile remains low, possibly out of respect to Guevara's surviving widow.

Haydée Tamara Bunke Bider, known as Tania the Guerrilla, is honoured in Cuba for her death in Bolivia in 1967.

24. MONUMENTO A ANTONIO MACEO (SANTIAGO DE CUBA)

Plaza de la Revolución, opposite the bus terminal, at Avenidas de las Américas and de los Libertadores

This enormous bronze statue of Antonio Maceo on horseback, designed by Alberto Lescay Merencio and erected in 1991, is easily the most impressive modern structure in eastern Cuba. Adjoining an empty park for mass gatherings, the Bronze Titan is depicted on a rearing horse, beckoning others to follow him. This equestrian masterpiece was erected

The largest modern monument in eastern Cuba is this towering statue of Antonio Maceo in Santiago de Cuba's Plaza de la Revolución.

for the Fourth Congress of the Communist Party of Cuba in 1991, along with the nearby Teatro Heredia where Castro has given his annual July 26 address to the nation. This final fling of architectural optimism (coincidental with the withdrawal of Soviet aid) also gave rise to the Antonio Maceo Airport and the remarkably ugly but modernist Hotel Santiago de Cuba. There is an eternal flame for Maceo as well as 23 enormous machetes in the ground to recall his battles and to recognize March 23, 1878, the day he resumed his war against the Spanish after opposing the Zanjón Treaty with Spain.

25. CASTILLO DEL MORRO

Ten kilometres southwest of Santiago de Cuba

Castillo de San Pedro del Morro, commonly known as El Morro, protects the southern entrance to Bahía de Santiago de Cuba. The romantic site attracts Cuban lovers at sunset and tour buses all day long. The tourists dutifully trudge through the castle's so-called Museum of Piracy. First built in 1633, destroyed by pirate Henry Morgan, then rebuilt, El Morro was designed in 1587 by the Italian

A collection of rusty cannons are on display at Castillo del Morro.

military engineer Giovanni Bautista Antonelli, who also created the Castillo del Morro in Havana. Towering 60 metres above the ocean on a rocky bluff, Santiago's El Morro is a vivid reminder that this city was successfully attacked by pirates such as Morgan and Jacques de Sores. The castle's inner chambers were used to house African slaves in transit.

26. GRANJITA SIBONEY

Approximately 16 kilometres east of Santiago de Cuba on the road to the beach resort area of Baconao

Fidel Castro and most of his rebels stayed at this farmhouse prior to attacking the Moncada Barracks on July 26, 1953. (Others resided downtown at the Hotel Rex and at another hotel.) The guns were hidden in a well. To commemorate the early-morning raid, there are 26 monuments along the highway between this museum and Santiago de Cuba.

Fidel Castro hid weapons in this well at Granjita Siboney near Santiago de Cuba before his failed attack in 1953 on the Moncada Army Barracks.

Many of Castro's 119-member force became lost on the winding streets of the city and never reached their destination. Only six died in combat; another 55 were killed in captivity. Abel Santamaría was one of the two men who rented the farmhouse, ostensibly because they wanted to have a chicken ranch. Few rebels knew the nature of the mission Castro had planned. When told of the plans, only two chose not to participate. After the attack failed, the police found these two noncombatants and brutally murdered them.

27. BASÍLICA DE NUESTRA SEÑORA DEL COBRE
Twenty kilometres northwest of Santiago de Cuba

The Virgin of Copper pilgrimage site, built with stones from Italy, is Cuba's only *basílica menor* and is home to a small Virgen de Caridad (Charity) statuette, proclaimed to be Cuba's national saint in 1916. Supposedly found in the waters of Bahía de Nipe by two Spanish boys and a black youth in 1606, this Madonna figurine doubles as the Yoruba goddess of love, Ochún, always depicted in yellow in keeping with

The patron saint of Cuba is the black Madonna found in the Basílica de Nuestra Señora del Cobre, situated above the oldest continuously operating open-pit mine in the Americas.

the Santería faith brought by slaves from Africa. A potent hybrid of African mysticism and Catholicism, the Virgin of Charity is worthy of being called the Lourdes of Cuba. Penitents bring letters and personal mementos to give thanks to the Virgin for her help; many of these are on display. The Virgin of Charity has attracted millions of pilgrims and admirers, including Ernest Hemingway, Antonio Maceo, Thomas Merton, Castro's mother, and Pope John Paul II (in 1998). Even for the irreligious, this is an inspiring and relatively unspoiled haven for faith and healing. Mountain breezes waft through the church. You leave changed.

Alberto Lescay Merencio's modernist sculpture *El Cimarrón* pays homage to runaway slaves.

28. MONUMENTO AL CIMARRÓN

El Cobre, to the right of the entrance to the open-pit mine

Few tourists and pilgrims to El Cobre see or even know about *El Cimarrón*. The hard-to-find, six-metre monument that celebrates runaway slaves is above the village of El Cobre. Countless thousands of slaves died at the copper mine that gapes directly below. Still operating, it's the oldest European-initiated open-pit mine in the Western Hemisphere, dating back to 1530. Atrocities committed against the black slaves in Cuba continued for more than three centuries. (Cuba was the second-to-last colony in the Americas to outlaw slavery; Brazil under the Portuguese was the last.) This new monument, designed by Alberto Lescay Merencio and completed in 1997, is part of a UNESCO initiative to raise awareness about slavery. It was commissioned by Doudou Dienne, a Senegalese man from Paris who wanted to understand the fate of his ancestors who were taken from West Africa. Dienne personally donated $10,000 to initiate the *El Cimarrón* project. Cuban and UNESCO authorities wanted it erected nearer to the famous Virgin of Copper church, but a local Santería spirit guide or *babalao*, Juan González Pérez, received contrary instructions from a spirit. González worked closely with both Dienne and Lescay Merencio to create the site, partially completed by century's end. González's Santería shrine is about halfway up the hill. Don't disturb any of his bones, symbolic items, or the sacred ceiba tree he planted. Everything has a purpose. The hidden hilltop location has one very obvious strategic advantage: it's higher than the Roman Catholic basilica.

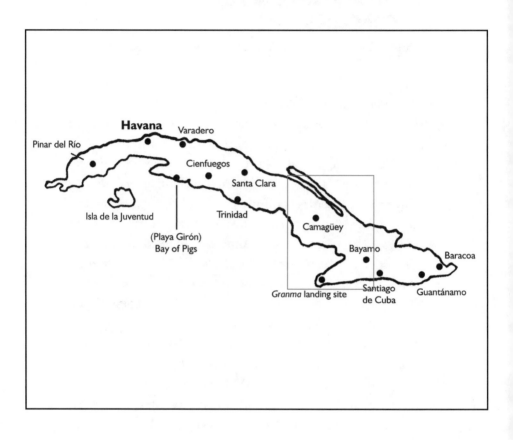

Havana

Pinar del Río

Varadero

Cienfuegos

Santa Clara

Isla de la Juventud

Trinidad

(Playa Girón)
Bay of Pigs

Camagüey

Bayamo

Baracoa

Granma landing site

Santiago
de Cuba

Guantánamo

WEST AND NORTH OF SANTIAGO DE CUBA

After he landed at Playa de las Coloradas in the *Granma* in December 1956, Fidel Castro used the Sierra Maestra as a base of operations for his revolution.

A lthough usually given short shrift in the tourist guides, this section of Cuba is well worth visiting, even for a circular jaunt, because it's the area where Fidel Castro's revolution, as well as Carlos Manuel de Céspedes's republican rebellion, gave rise to independence from foreign control. This region is also the birthplace of Celia Sánchez, the most remarkable woman in Cuban history.

The monument at El Uvero immortalizes Fidel Castro's first major military success on May 28, 1957.

29. EL UVERO
Approximately 110 kilometres west of Santiago de Cuba, 23 kilometres west of Chivirico, on the coastal highway

On May 28, 1957, Fidel Castro's ragtag revolutionary landing party had its first major military success here. Castro's men vanquished 55 of Fulgencio Batista's soldiers at a remote army outpost. This victory not only gained desperately needed supplies, it signalled to the rest of the country, and to Castro's soldiers, that their invasion force could be taken seriously as a liberation movement and not just another of Castro's cock-eyed publicity stunts. Two red trucks captured by the rebels are on display near the roadway; the monument is flanked by two rows of royal palms, the national tree. The local people of El Uvero are proud *Fidelístas* and will tell you that Castro fired the first shot from a hillside to the right of the monument.

30. PICO TURQUINO
West of El Uvero, approachable from Las Cuevas on the south coast

Cuba's highest mountain (1,972 metres) has long been climbed by Cuban patriots. Celia Sánchez ascended Pico Turquino with her father as a homage to José Martí; Fidel Castro came here from his headquarters near Villa Santo Domingo, to the north, during his guerrilla campaign; in the 1960s Cuban trainees were forced to climb this peak repeatedly to prove their dedication to the revolutionary cause. Permission to climb the mountain must now be obtained at least 30 days in advance, with a letter explaining the purpose of the visit. From the roadway it's easy to see the country's second-highest peak, Pico Cuba (1,872

Celia Sánchez and her father climbed Cuba's highest mountain and erected a bust of José Martí at the summit.

metres); Pico Turquino is behind it. Mules are available for the ascent. There seems to be precious little reason to restrict entrance beyond Castro's desire to mythologize Pico Turquino into his private Mount Olympus. It takes about six hours to climb to the summit at an easy pace, and four hours to descend.

31. MUSEO DE LA PLATA

Five kilometres west of Las Cuevas, 30 kilometres east of Marea del Portillo

Fidel Castro's first major victory over the enemy occurred here in 1957. Beside the river a three-room museum immortalizes that encounter. This site is not to be confused with Comandancia de la Plata, Castro's personal headquarters in the mountains near Villa Santo Domingo, where Fidel and his rebels began to broadcast on Radio Rebelde in February 1958. Like many populists, Castro has been extraordinarily skillful at using media ever since his university days. He has long manipulated and befriended foreign correspondents and literati, most notably *New York Times* correspondent Herbert Matthews and intellectuals such as Jean-Paul Sartre and Gabriel García Márquez. Some foreign female journalists haven't been immune to his dynamic personality, as well. Identifying the crude roadway used for entrance to this worthwhile museum is impossible without local help. There are some rare photos and documents, including a list of

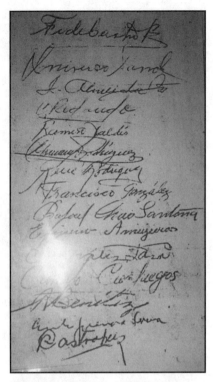

In the Museo de la Plata the signatures of the 15 revolutionaries who survived the *Granma* landing are on display. Fidel Castro's signature is at the top; Che Guevara's is second from the bottom.

signatures for the 15 men of Castro's invasion force who survived the *Granma* landing.

32. MUSEO CELIA SÁNCHEZ
Pilón, 90 kilometres southwest of Manzanillo

Celia Sánchez, the most influential Cuban woman in history, lived here with her father, a liberal intellectual and medical doctor, from 1940 to 1956. Here she also met local resistance movement leader Frank País and planned an

Celia Sánchez planned the uprising in Santiago de Cuba with Frank País during a meeting in her father's backyard in Pilón.

uprising. In the backyard is the tree under which they conspired to support Fidel Castro's invasion. Her former bedroom in this converted museum has an extensive and rare collection of Celia Sánchez photos. Employed by the sugar company in Pilón, Sánchez's father used this house for his medical practice. Outside is the original tree house in a mango tree where Sánchez taught herself English while her father attended to his patients.

33. *GRANMA* LANDING SITE
Los Cayuelos, Playa de las Coloradas, near Niquero

A concrete walkway leads through a dense mangrove swamp, approximately one-and-a-half kilometres long, to the landing area where 81 seasick Cuban insurrectionists arrived from Mexico on December 2, 1956, led by Fidel Castro. Their transportation was the overcrowded yacht *Granma*. Instead of wading ashore on a nearby sandy beach, the rebels were stranded, lost, hungry, and overdue. A little jetty marks the spot. The tiny Playa de las Coloradas

A walkway leads to the shoreline where the *Granma* dropped off Fidel Castro and his rebels on December 2, 1956.

museum on the roadway mainly boasts a full-size replica of the *Granma* in an otherwise empty parking lot, plus a rare first photo of Castro upon his arrival.

34. CELIA SÁNCHEZ BIRTHPLACE

Media Luna, Calle Paúl Podio No. 111

In this clapboard house in Media Luna, Celia Sánchez Manduley was born on May 8, 1920. From 1940 to 1956 she lived in Pilón and organized the network of support for Fidel Castro. She became his essential personal secretary and lover in the Sierra Maestra. Having been the dutiful daughter to her father, Sánchez switched her emotional allegiance to the charismatic Fidel. She nonetheless retained her intellectual independence. With her liberal integrity and her organization-

Celia Sánchez, described as the "most beautiful native flower of the revolution," was Fidel Castro's adviser and one of his staunchest supporters.

al will, she often steered Castro's enormous ego. A Celia Sánchez monument in Manzanillo pays tribute by describing her as *Lo mas hermosa y autóctona flor de la revolución* (the most beautiful native flower of the revolution). It is entirely plausible that the Cuban revolution would never have succeeded without her.

35. LA DEMAJAGUA BELL

Ten kilometres south of Manzanillo

The 136-kilogram Demajagua Bell, a national treasure, was brought in 1947 to the University of Havana by law student Fidel Castro and other dissidents to be rung during anti-government demonstrations. When authorities removed the bell, Castro took to the airwaves in protest, making his name widely known to the Cuban public for the first time. This same bell was used at this location by Carlos Manuel de

Carlos Manuel de Céspedes freed his slaves on October 10, 1868, ringing this plantation bell and marking the birth of the modern Cuban independence movement.

Céspedes to free his slaves on October 10, 1868. The museum has a remnant of the first flag of Cuban independence and a freakishly three-pronged royal palm, the national tree.

36. MANZANILLO TRAIN STATION
Fifty kilometres west of Bayamo

Labour leader Jesús Menéndez Larrondo was murdered here on the train platform in 1948. Reputedly incorruptible, Menéndez was a thorn in the side of the local sugar barons for his role in collecting sugar workers' grievances. Manzanillo was home to Cuba's first Communist cell in the 1920s and also democratically elected a communist mayor, Paquito Rosales, in the 1940s.

A plaque at the Manzanillo Train Station memorializes Jesús Menéndez Larrondo, Cuba's first martyr for communism, who was killed by local sugar barons in 1948.

Left-wing opposition to the sugar and cigar plantation owners, as well as to the enormously powerful United Fruit Company, was extremely dangerous. Angel Castro built his fortune in eastern Cuba by working for and with the United Fruit Company.

37. TOWN SQUARE (YARA)
Twenty-three kilometres east of Manzanillo

Confusion continued for centuries as to whether Taíno chief Hatuey was burned alive at Baracoa or in faraway Yara. At the end of the 20th century the town of Yara commissioned Wailfredo Milanez to make a statue of Hatuey adjoining the square to support its rival claim. The evidence Hatuey died in Yara was uncovered by Cuban historian Hortencia Pichardo in the Seville archives. In 1985 she published her findings in a book called *Where Did Hatuey Die? (Donde que immoledo Hatuey?)*. According to Pichardo, Hatuey had hoped to mobilize the Taíno population near Bayamo, but that place was chosen by Diego Velázquez for the second Spanish town site in Cuba. A 1992 maritime expedition subsequently proved Hatuey's migrations to Yara could have been accomplished by reaching present-day Manzanillo in dugout canoes. A hand-held model of Hatuey's Christ-like statue can be seen at the nearby museum.

This Christ-like sculpture in Yara's town square poignantly recalls the execution of Taíno chief Hatuey in 1512.

Fidel Castro and Celia Sánchez, seen here in the Sierra Maestra during the late 1950s, were lovers as well as co-revolutionaries.

38. COMANDANCIA DE LA PLATA

Approximately 40 kilometres south of Yara

The tiny town of Villa Santo Domingo served as the mostly closed gateway to Fidel Castro's main headquarters during the Sierra Maestra campaign. It is sometimes possible to obtain written permission to approach this shrine on foot. The mountainous hideout is reachable by trail from Alto del Naranjo, five kilometres from Villa Santo Domingo, going southwest. Three kilometres later is the rebel command post where Radio Rebelde made its first broadcasts. There is an official museum, a field hospital, and Castro's private bedroom. In the Gran Parque Nacional Sierra Maestra is the famous ceiba tree under which the rebels sometimes met. Surmounting Cuban red tape and officialdom will likely prove more arduous than the actual hike in the rainforest.

39. MUSEO MUNICIPAL (YARA)

Calle Grito de Yara No. 107

Carlos Manuel de Céspedes led his first successful battle against Spanish troops at Yara on October 11, 1868. In the museum near the square is a depiction of Céspedes's triumphant arrival in Yara by Bayamo artist Labrada Varela. Here he proclaimed his radical republican ideals with his famous *Grito de Yara* (Yara Declaration). The museum also honours Yara-born Delsa Esther Puebla Viltre who left

Having served with Fidel Castro in the Sierra Maestra in the 1950s, Yara's Delsa Esther Puebla Viltre became Cuba's only female brigadier general in 1996.

home to join Fidel Castro's revolutionary camp in the Sierra Maestra at age 16. "Dada" was elevated to captain by the end of the campaign, a symbol that women could play leadership roles in the revolution. Long prominent in Cuban affairs, she was promoted by Castro to the position of Cuba's only female *general de brigada* (brigadier general) on July 24, 1996.

40. PARQUE CÉSPEDES (BAYAMO)

With his ever-present recognition of Cuban history, Fidel Castro chose this square in Bayamo as the site for a massive anti-American rally in March 2000 to protest the retention of the Cuban boy Elián González in Florida. The boy was later released to the custody of his Cuban father. Just as Castro declared Cuba's independence from the town

In March 2000 Fidel Castro chose Parque Céspedes in Bayamo to mount a mammoth anti-American protest against the retention of the Cuban boy Elián González in Florida.

hall in Santiago de Cuba in 1959, Carlos Manuel de Céspedes first announced Cuba's independence from Spain at this town hall in Cuba's second-oldest city on October 20, 1868. It was here that Céspedes signed a declaration to abolish slavery gradually in Cuba. Céspedes, a lawyer, also helped to compose the first anthem for independence. The current anthem of Cuba was composed by Perucho Figueredo, a Bayamo lawyer and landowner who supported the Republican cause. A monument honours Figueredo in the town square. There is also an official "Hymn Square" adjoining nearby Iglesia Parroquial Mayor de San Salvador where "La Bayamesa" was first sung by 12 women in 1868. The Cuban anthem begins, "To combat run, people of Bayamo." Hence Bayamo retains special significance for all loyal Cubans.

41. CARLOS MANUEL DE CÉSPEDES BIRTHPLACE

Bayamo, west end of Parque Céspedes at Calle Maceo No. 57

The Bayamo birthplace of Carlos Manuel de Céspedes beside the provincial museum contains the sword sent to Céspedes by sympathetic followers in the United States; family relics such as kitchen pots, furniture, and an enormous wooden bowl for grinding coffee; and letters, Céspedes's legal texts, and the printing press on which he printed *Cubana Libre*, the first independent newspaper in Cuba. Céspedes was born here on April 18, 1819. A poet, lawyer, and planter, he freed his slaves and was soon joined by

Poet, lawyer, and planter Carlos Manuel de Céspedes was killed in 1873 in an early Cuban bid to win independence from Spain.

1,500 men seeking independence from Spanish control. He was elected president by his supporters, then deposed after an internal feud. Céspedes was killed in battle in 1873.

42. MUSEO ÑICO LÓPEZ

Bayamo, south of Parque Céspedes on Calle Abihail González

At 5:15 a.m. on July 26, 1953, to coincide with Fidel Castro's attack on the Moncada Army Barracks, the happy-go-lucky, tall, and thin Antonio "Ñico" López led an attack of 21 *moncadistas* on the Bayamo Barracks. The rebels didn't realize the front gate would be locked at night; 12 of them were killed. López was injured, took refuge in Guatemala's embassy in Havana, and escaped to Guatemala where he befriended Che Guevara. It was López who gave Guevara his nickname, Che, meaning "Hey, you." Later, in Mexico City in 1955, López introduced the Argentine doctor to Castro. López was killed during the landing of the *Granma* and remains one of the best-loved martyrs of the revolution.

43. DOS RÍOS
Fifty-two kilometres east of Bayamo

This is Cuba's Golgotha, a shrine to the Cuban tradition of martyrdom that infuses Cuban political history. Here José Martí died in battle on May 19, 1895. He was instructed to stay at the rear of a minor fight but foolishly charged forward and was quickly killed. There is an enormous parking lot, empty, and a conspicuous but not inspired obelisk. The monument is most remarkable for the government's concerted effort to grow green grass in a nation with only one-and-a-half golf courses. Like Christ, Martí is known to have died for others and his repu-

An obelisk marks the scene of José Martí's death in battle against the Spanish on May 19, 1895, at Dos Ríos.

tation is immortal as a result. Proceed east from Bayamo to Jiguani, then take the northeast turnoff toward Las Palmas. Keep going until you cross Río Cauto twice. On the right you'll arrive at Dos Ríos.

44. HOMONGOLONGO
Twenty-seven kilometres northwest of Santiago de Cuba

On the road above El Cobre is a tank captured from Fulgencio Batista's soldiers on December 8, 1958, in a battle led by a mulatto songwriter turned soldier, Juan Almeida, one of the men who survived the *Granma* invasion and regrouped in the Sierra Maestra. Almeida's association with Fidel Castro dates back to the Moncada Army Barracks attack. In May 1955 Almeida was famously photographed striding out of prison with a defiant Castro after Batista declared an amnesty. As one of only three army *commandantes* directly below Commander in Chief Castro in rank, Almeida has remained active and popular in Cuba's government. Some Cubans might claim Cuba's greatest progress since 1959 has been the country's determined shift away from centuries of racial prejudice against blacks. Almeida has long been the most high-ranking black in the Cuban power structure.

45. FINCA MANACAS (BIRÁN)
Twenty kilometres southwest of Mayarí, 60 kilometres southeast of Holguín

Off-limits to most visitors, permanently guarded and barricaded with a chain, here the old Castro general store is preserved along with a house on wooden pilings where Fidel Castro was born on August 13, 1926. Having leased land from the United Fruit Company in 1910, Castro's Spanish-born father, Angel, gradually became wealthy growing sugarcane, operating a sawmill, and owning a nickel mine. In the process he provided a "one-man rule" model for his son. The graves of Castro's parents, Angel and Lina, are near the entrance, not far from the remains of a rudimentary school.

Fidel Castro was born here at Finca Manacas near Birán on August 13, 1926.

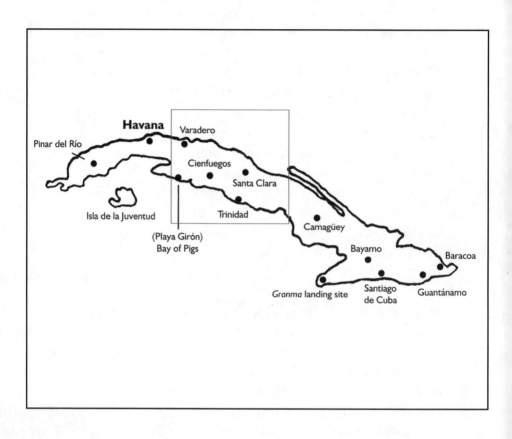

Havana

Pinar del Río

Varadero

Cienfuegos

Santa Clara

Isla de la Juventud

Trinidad

(Playa Girón)
Bay of Pigs

Camagüey

Bayamo

Baracoa

Granma landing site

Santiago
de Cuba

Guantánamo

CENTRAL CUBA

The opulent homes, stately religious buildings (including the former convent of San Francisco de Asís in the background), and lovely courtyards and cobblestoned streets of Trinidad were built thanks to the wealth generated by the once-numerous sugar mills and plantations in the region.

The chief attraction in Central Cuba is Trinidad, the country's third-oldest city and a photographer's paradise. This area also recognizes Che Guevara's decisive defeat of Fulgencio Batista's soldiers at Santa Clara and Cuba's trouncing of CIA-trained troops at Playa Girón on Bahía de Cochinos, known in English as the Bay of Pigs. Frequently overlooked in this region but not without its charms is Cienfuegos, Cuba's seventh-largest city.

The Armoured Train Monument commemorates the decisive battle between Che Guevara's insurgents and Fulgencio Batista's soldiers on December 29, 1958.

46. ARMOURED TRAIN MONUMENT

Santa Clara, 276 kilometres east of Havana, on Calle Independencia

Che Guevara's forces won a decisive battle by derailing an armoured train here on December 29, 1958. This victory convinced Fulgencio Batista to flee Cuba. Batista had tried to stop the rebel advance with 3,500 soldiers in Santa Clara, to be supported by an armoured train loaded with ammunition and communications equipment. Guevara, with only 340 fighters, had a section of rail track pulled up by tractors. After a three-day battle, government soldiers tried to escape on the armoured train, but three of the cars derailed when the train hit the missing track. A few weeks before in Santa Clara, Guevara picked up a local schoolteacher named Aleida March in his jeep. In the midst of the battle for Santa Clara he realized he was in love with the woman. She became his second wife and bore him four children.

47. MONUMENTO A ERNESTO "CHE" GUEVARA

Santa Clara, in Plaza de la Revolución

The seven-metre bronze statue of Che Guevara erected in 1988 has an adjoining exhibit for his assumed lover Haydée Tamara Bunke Bider (Tania the Guerrilla), who was killed in Bolivia on August 31, 1967. On October 9, 1967, Guevara was also killed in Bolivia, and his remains were unearthed in July 1997. Tania's body was found in September 1988. Both were buried in unmarked graves near the town of Vallegrande, 772 kilometres southeast of La Paz, about a kilometre apart. Tania's remains were brought

Images of Che Guevara such as this roadside billboard are everywhere in Cuba.

to Santa Clara to coincide with the 40th anniversary of Fidel Castro's revolution and were entombed in the presence of her mother, Nadia Bunke, a Cuban resident. Guevara continues to be venerated as the Cuban alternative to Jesus Christ. For an in-depth, eye-opening understanding of Guevara, consult Jon Lee Anderson's exhaustive 1997 biography *Che Guevara: A Revolutionary Life*.

48. FOOTBALL STADIUM (SANTA CLARA)

Pope John Paul II's first Mass in Cuba was celebrated here on February, 22, 1998. About 40,000 Cubans took advantage of free transportation and a morning off work to attend. Beer sales were respectfully curtailed, but religious paraphernalia wasn't sold. Fidel Castro's concession to allow the pope to visit Cuba and try to regain some of his flock—millions of whom in Latin America have transferred their allegiance to Fundamentalist Christian factions financed by right-wing ministries in the United States—was a cynical attempt to curry favour with world opinion. In return for his invitation the pope criticized the U.S. trade embargo.

Pope John Paul II's first Catholic Mass in Cuba was held on a hillside above the Santa Clara football stadium.

When Castro was young, his mother, Lina, was a fervent Catholic as well as a devotee of Santería spiritualism. During the revolution, Castro sometimes wore a small medallion of the Virgin of Copper sent to him by a young girl in Santiago de Cuba—not given to him by his mother as is generally believed—but he has never considered himself to be religious.

49. WATCHTOWER (MANACA IZNAGA)
Sixteen kilometres east of Trinidad

On his 18th-century estate Pedro Iznaga became one of Cuba's richest men by trading in slaves. A 44-metre tower next to the hacienda was used to watch the slaves. This watchtower, now a tourist attraction, stands as a sobering reminder of a colonial economy dependent on slavery and cruelty for centuries. Aristocratic homes in Havana routinely had 20 or 30 slaves; wealthy homes had more than 100.

Slave manacles were used to control many thousands of Africans who provided the cheap labour that served as the foundation of sugar fortunes in Cuba.

Punishments were severe. Many slaves committed suicide by eating earth, hanging themselves, taking poison, or suffocating themselves. The English conqueror of Havana, George Keppel, third earl of Albemarle, greatly boosted the importance of slavery in Cuba when he sold the 1,200 slaves he used to take Havana in 1762.

50. MUSEO NACIONAL DE LA LUCHA CONTRA BANDIDOS

Trinidad, Calle Echerri No. 59 at Piro Guinart

Formerly the 18th-century convent of San Francisco de Asís, this building was transformed in 1984 into the National Museum of the Struggle Against Counterrevolutionaries, specifically those in the Sierra del Escambray who opposed Fidel Castro's ascension to power in the 1960s. The foundations date from 1522. Beneath the distinctive yellow tower are attractions such as Che Guevara's hammock and an American U–2 spy plane that was shot down over Cuba. The bell tower affords

The bell tower of the former convent of San Francisco de Asís now rests atop a museum that celebrates the fight against counterrevolutionaries.

a spectacular view. Trinidad, Cuba's third-oldest city, became a UNESCO World Heritage Site in 1988.

51. NUCLEAR POWER PLANT
West side of Bahía de Cienfuegos

The remains of Cuba's most ambitious thermoelectric power plant are a grim reminder of Cuba's uneasy reliance on Soviet technology and aid. All over Cuba there are Cuban technicians cursing Russian machines and inventing new ways to fix the country's inferior Soviet-based infrastructure. Educated in the Soviet Union, Fidel Castro's only legitimate son, Fidelito, was one of Cuba's leading nuclear scientists in the 1980s. His public profile dropped considerably after the Soviets severed their extensive support in 1991.

52. CASTILLO DE JAGUA
Western mouth of Bahía de Cienfuegos

Predating the founding of Cienfuegos, Cuba's seventh-largest city, the foundations for Castillo de Jagua were begun by the Spanish in 1738 to protect the bay from pirates. After a hurricane destroyed a settlement called Fernandina de Jagua in 1825, present-day Cienfuegos was established in 1831. The city is home to Cuba's largest oil refinery; the Teatro Tomás Terry (where Enrico Caruso and Sarah Bernhardt performed); a botanical garden with one of the world's most varied collections of palm trees; and Paseo del Prado, the longest promenade in Cuba.

Built to combat pirates, the mid-18th-century Castillo de Jagua predates the founding of the city of Cienfuegos.

53. MUSEO PLAYA GIRÓN (BAY OF PIGS)

Eastern mouth of Bahía de Cochinos or Bay of Pigs

Outside this museum in the town of Playa Girón is a British Sea Fury aircraft that was used by Cubans to repel the invasion of approximately 1,300 CIA-sponsored mercenaries on April 17, 1961. Now touted as "the first defeat of U.S. imperialism in the Americas," the battle known in North America as the Bay of Pigs lasted 72 hours and resulted in the deaths of 200 counter-revolutionaries. The Cubans reputedly shot down 11 planes.

The Museo Playa Girón features exhibits concerning Cuba's defeat of counterrevolutionaries during the Bay of Pigs invasion in 1961.

Within a year there were more than 40,000 Soviet troops in Cuba. Between Playa Girón and Central Australia are roadside markers to honour the Cuban militia members who died during the battle.

54. SUGAR PLANT, CENTRAL AUSTRALIA

The oddly named plantation Central Australia doubled as Fidel Castro's military headquarters when he vanquished the infamous CIA-sponsored Bay of Pigs assault. A modest museum features a blurry photo of Castro leaping from the tank he used during the Bay of Pigs. The tank is on display outside the Museo de la Revolución in Havana. The importance of sugar, used for the rum industry, remains extreme. State socialism employs students each year to

Fidel Castro used this tank in the defence of his revolution at Playa Girón on the Bay of Pigs.

help with the sugar harvest, which is seen as an education-al opportunity. In their early teens almost all Cubans must leave home to attend rural schools and sleep in dormito-ries. Part of each day is devoted to conventional school work. During the rest of the day, the students are given a "hands-on" appreciation of the importance of sugar to the Cuban state. In 1970 Cubans were urged to produce a record sugar harvest of 10 million tonnes, an unrealistic initiative that failed. Castro asked the people for forgive-ness and, not surprisingly, he received it.

55. JOSÉ ANTONIO ECHEVERRÍA BIRTHPLACE
Cárdenas, 18 kilometres southeast of Varadero

This museum at Avenida 4 Este No. 560 in Cárdenas was the birthplace of student leader José Antonio Echeverría, who was killed by Fulgencio Batista's police in 1957. Equally noteworthy is the museum's display of the garrote used to execute General Narciso López by strangulation in 1851. López had led an unsuccessful annexation attempt by 600 American soldiers, mostly from Kentucky and Ohio. The general was nonetheless responsible for raising the first Cuban flag of independence here on May 19, 1850. Ironically the single star in its design was intentionally derivative of the flag of Texas. A plaque commemorates the flag-raising at Café La Dominica on Avenida Céspedes, near the Christopher Columbus statue. The original López flag is supposedly on display at the Museo de la Ciudad in Havana. An antique, tattered flag in the museum at the Céspedes plantation shows a slightly different one-star, 19th-century design.

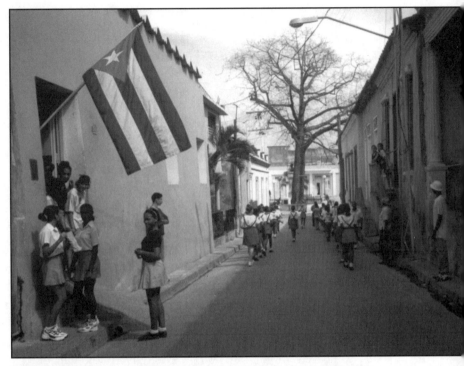

The Cuban flag, seen here in a Cárdenas street, was modelled on the Lone Star design of the Texas flag.

56. XANADU (DU PONT MANSION)

Varadero, 140 kilometres east of Havana

The equivalent of Mexico's Cancún, the thriving tourist Mecca of Varadero can be traced back to the purchase of 512 hectares of waterfront property by French-born chemical magnate Eleuthère Irénée Du Pont. Having made his fortune from manufacturing dynamite during World War I, Du Pont was able to acquire property for as little as four centavos per square metre. He built a lavish vacation house, now a restaurant and bed-and-breakfast. The former Du Pont mansion is surrounded by a new 18-hole golf course in an area not

Not exactly the Xanadu of Samuel Taylor Coleridge's *Kubla Khan* or Orson Welles's *Citizen Kane*, French-born chemical baron Eleuthère Irénée Du Pont's former mansion in Varadero is still a "stately pleasure-dome."

easily visited by Cubans. The exclusivity of Varadero's upscale section leads to the charge that Varadero practises tourist apartheid.

57. MARIEL BOATLIFT

Mariel, approximately 50 kilometres east of Havana

This coastal town gave rise to the Mariel boatlift consisting of hundreds of privately owned boats from Florida. The so-called Mariel Freedom Flotilla, largely financed by Cuban exiles, brought approximately 125,000 Cubans to Key West, 145 kilometres away, and Miami, 400 kilometres away, in 1980. It occurred after a Cuban bus driver drove his passengers through the gates of the Peruvian embassy and asked for political asylum. As retribution, Fidel Castro removed the embassy guard only to have 10,000 more Cubans enter the Peruvian grounds and seek protection. He decided to let malcontents flee the country, as well as thousands of homosexuals, criminals, and mental patients. The ongoing influx of Cuban refugees to the United States throughout the 1980s became so burdensome that, in 1994, the United States reversed its 1966 Cuban Adjustment Act to stop the *balseros* (rafters), many of whom never reached Florida. Since 1959 more than a million Cubans have left the island, either legally or illegally.

58. ERNEST HEMINGWAY'S FINCA LA VIGÍA

Twenty-four kilometres southeast of Havana

In 1940 Ernest Hemingway moved to Finca la Vigía in San Francisco de Paula. His third wife, Martha Gellhorn, found the house. They bought it for us$18,500 cash. Here Hemingway entertained some of Hollywood's elite such as Ava Gardner (who swam naked in the pool), Spencer Tracy, Lana Turner, Errol Flynn, and Gary Cooper. The villa is now an impressive museum, with Hemingway's stuffed big-game heads, firearms, thousands of books, Victrola, and countless knickknacks on view. Papa loathed Fulgencio Batista and his "murderous tyranny." He once wrote to a friend: "I believe completely in the historical necessity of the Cuban revolution." But Hemingway never used his enormous public clout as the world's most famous writer to help the fledgling Castro regime.

Ernest Hemingway's swimming pool at Finca la Vigía, his former villa outside Havana, was once graced by Hollywood celebrities, including actress Ava Gardner.

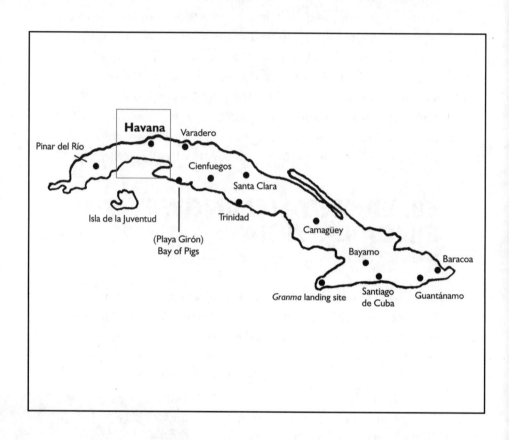

Havana

Pinar del Río

Varadero

Cienfuegos

Santa Clara

Isla de la Juventud

Trinidad

(Playa Girón)
Bay of Pigs

Camagüey

Bayamo

Baracoa

Granma landing site

Santiago
de Cuba

Guantánamo

HAVANA

Cabs come in all shapes and sizes in Havana, including the city's distinctive yellow coco-taxis.

Havana is almost five centuries old and is home to more than two million people. The city is divided into 15 municipalities, which include Habana Vieja, Centro Habana, Plaza de la Revolución (which incorporates Vedado), Playa, Marianao, and Cerro. Locations in Habana Vieja, or Old Havana, are within easy walking distance. Most people gravitate to Plaza de Armas along Calle Obispo, a pedestrian-only mall that connects the venerable square to the José Martí statue and Hotel Inglaterra, the oldest hotel in Cuba, on Paseo de Martí (formerly called the Prado). Bizarre sites such as the Russian Embassy are farther afield. Take a taxi.

Although not the original ceiba,
this tree marks the legendary spot
where the reestablished Havana was
founded in 1519.

59. CEIBA TREE
Plaza de Armas, eastern end of Calle Obispo

This ceiba tree marks the founding of the largest city in the Caribbean and Central America by Pánfilo de Narváez. According to legend, the town's first Mass and town meeting were held beneath a ceiba tree in 1519. Every year at midnight on November 15, to mark Havana's birth date, the minister of culture and other Cubans walk silently around this tree three times to make a wish. This particular ceiba tree was planted in soil from various countries of the Americas. Next to it, on the fence, there is a small United Nations plaque officially declaring Habana Vieja a UNESCO World Heritage Site.

60. EL TEMPLETE (LITTLE TEMPLE)
Eastern side of Plaza de Armas

After its Spartan beginnings, Havana became extraordinary wealthy, but today thousands of mansions and public buildings remain in varying degrees of disrepair. The first to incorporate neoclassicism was El Templete, the Little Temple, in the shade of the ceiba tree. It was completed in the style of a Doric temple in 1827. Inside El Templete are early 19th-century frescoes by Jean-Baptiste Vermay that depict Havana's inception. Nearby at Calle Obrapía No. 158 near Calle Mercaderes, the much older Casa de la Obra Pía from the 17th century is famous for its grandeur but also because one of its owners, Don Martin, bequeathed the interest from a 100,000-peso trust fund to dowering five orphan girls per year, thereby giving rise to the street name

Inside the Doric-style El Templete are frescoes by Jean-Baptiste Vermay, including this one portraying the establishment of Havana.

Obrapía (pious act). The list of remarkable colonial homes in Havana is almost endless. Governor Tacón's Quinta de los Molinos, for instance, is a grand summer residence of the 18th century. Despite millions being spent each year to preserve Habana Vieja, about 300 buildings collapse every year.

61. CASTILLO DE LA REAL FUERZA

Northeastern side of Plaza de Armas

Next to Havana's oldest square is the oldest fortress still standing in Cuba. It was begun in 1558 and completed in 1577. A famous bronze weathervane sculpture called *La Giraldilla*, made by local artisan Jerónimo Martínez Pinzón, was placed atop the fortress in 1632. The story goes that Doña Inés de Bobadilla became Cuba's first female governor in 1539 after her husband, Hernando de

Soto, left for Florida in search of the Fountain of Youth. For four years she longed for his return, gazing out to sea. Her vigil ended when news arrived that de Soto had been buried in Mississippi. One of Havana's most enduring symbols, *La Giraldilla* commemorates the governess's vigil. It was modelled on a similar statue in Seville, Spain, and is often said to represent the spirit of the city. The spire now seen atop the castle is a replica of the original, which is kept in the nearby Museo de la Ciudad.

Atop Castillo de la Real Fuerza, a replica of *La Giraldilla* honours Cuba's first female governor.

62. MUSEO DE LA CIUDAD

Western side of Plaza de Armas

The Treaty of Paris that placed Cuba under American control was signed here in 1898. As well as the original *La Giraldilla* weathervane, the museum has an extraordinary mural of Antonio Maceo's death, erotic prints depicting Greek gods, a 19th-century fire engine, furnishings, portraits, dungeons, cock-fighting spurs, a sunlit 1862 statue of Christopher Columbus, and wooden cobbles that date back to 1791—because in those days it wouldn't do to disturb the sleep of Governor Luis de Las Casas, who lived here.

There are a few delights in the Antique Automobile Museum, including revolutionary Vilma Espín's jeep.

63. ANTIQUE AUTOMOBILE MUSEUM

Calle Oficios No. 13

Next to cigars, Ernest Hemingway, and the Buena Vista Social Club, the best-known aspect of Cuban culture is functional old cars. This dusty museum's cramped collection of antique automobiles includes a 1902 Cadillac as well as "modern" American cars that were driven by Che Guevara and Camilo Cienfuegos. History buffs who aren't car buffs might like to find the unmarked jeep that was driven by Vilma Espín, the high-society daughter turned radical. The streets of Havana became an open-air museum for automobiles when the United States began imposing trade sanctions against Cuba in the 1960s. Many Cuban cars appear to be American originals, but most are kept on the road due to the remarkable ability of Cubans to improvise with non-American parts. In much earlier times Cuba's aristocracy had noblesse oblige in their *volantas*, scattering pedestrians and animals alike; today's motorists continue the tradition of treating anyone walking as a second-class citizen. Pedestrians use the streets at their peril.

64. EL CASERÓN DEL TANGO

Casa Garibaldi at Calle Jústiz No. 21 off Calle Oficios

The novelist Gabriel García Márquez, a friend of Fidel Castro, has said that the Cuban people like to dance more than any other people. That's an exaggeration, but it supports the controversial claim that Cuba, not Argentina, originated the tango. Little publicized, this tango house offers the real thing, professional dancers as well as Cubans dancing for pleasure, across from the Casa de la Comedia theatre. Other dance forms associated with Cuba are the flamenco, the rumba, the derivative mambo (an American-based hybrid), the more simplistic chachacha, the bolero, the more upper-class danzón, and the conga. The last is a dance said to have been originated by African slaves with shackles on their feet.

A couple does what comes natural in El Caserón del Tango.

Ernest Hemingway met Fidel Castro only once—at the Ernest Hemingway
International Billfish Competition that Castro won in 1960.

65. HOTEL AMBOS MUNDOS

Calle Obispo No. 153

Ernest Hemingway liked to escape from matrimony to room
511 of this hotel (recently refurbished) where he drank, wrote,
and womanized. It's one of three tourist sites within Habana
Viejo that depend on connections to Hemingway. Papa drank
his *mojitos* at nearby La Bodeguita del Medio, west of Catedral
de San Cristóbal de La Habana on Calle Empedrado No. 207,
and his daiquiris at El Floridita, east of Parque Central on Calle
Obispo. Some 20 kilometres west of Havana is the Marina
Hemingway, home to the Ernest Hemingway International
Billfish Competition held annually in May. One of the reasons
Hemingway is officially venerated in Cuba is that Fidel Castro
once participated in Papa's fishing derby and caught the
biggest fish in 1960. Hemingway presented Castro with the
tournament's first prize. It was their only meeting.

José Martí was born here in 1853 and killed in battle 42 years later.

66. JOSÉ MARTÍ BIRTHPLACE
Calle Leonor Pérez No. 314

On a street since renamed to honour his mother, José Martí y Pérez, the Apostle of Independence, was born on January 28, 1853. At 16 he published *La Patria Libre* and was accused of treason. After six months of forced labour, he went into exile until 1878. Following his second deportation to Spain, Martí joined the Cuban exile community in New York City and remained in the United States for 15 years. He founded the Cuban Revolutionary Party in 1892 with Máximo Gómez as supreme commander. Martí was killed during his first battle on May 19, 1895. The birthplace (see photo on previous page) was made into a museum in 1925.

67. LA JUNTA
Central Train Station, on Calle Egido, across from Martí birthplace

On display in a train station that opened in 1912 is La Junta, the oldest (1840) locomotive in Latin America. La Junta is a standard-gauge 4-2-2 that was used by the Matanzas Railway and preserved in 1900. Having initiated railways in 1837 prior to Spain, Cuba maintained countless 100-year-old narrow- and standard-gauge steam engines throughout the 20th century. An old electric train built by the Hershey Chocolate Company remained operational from Havana to Matanzas as part of the mostly dieselized national railway system Ferrocarriles de Cuba (FCC). Used mainly for tourists, the oldest operational locomotive is the R. M. Vilena's coal-burning 0-4-2T No. 1112, which was built in 1878. A 1919 Baldwin Mogul steam train has also been reactivated to carry tourists near

The oldest locomotive in Latin America, La Junta, is on display in Havana's Central Railway Station.

Trinidad. To reinvigorate Cuba's essential rail service, Canada sold 50 Montreal-made MX-624 locomotives to Cuba in 1975.

68. DECLARATION OF CUBAN SOCIALISM

Near the entrance to Nécropolis Cristóbal Colon at the corner of Calles 23 and 12

A small plaque marks the spot where Fidel Castro first formally announced that his Cuban revolution was socialist on April 16, 1961. This declaration was made the day after CIA airplanes from Nicaragua bombed Cuban airfields, trying unsuccessfully to cripple the Cuban Air Force two days prior to the Bay of Pigs invasion. Seven Cuban airmen were killed during these preliminary airfield strikes. During his memorial speech here for the dead, Castro told the Cuban people, the United States, and the world that El Lídor Máximo was a dedicated socialist. Castro had always been enamoured of American society and was much less inclined toward left-wing extremism than both Che Guevara and his younger brother, Raúl Castro, but American-based aggression eventually forced him into this left-wing stance.

His beard may be white now and he may be packing more pounds, but Fidel Castro still irks the United States with his stubborn independent direction.

69. MIRACLE WOMAN
Nécropolis Cristóbal Colón

Of the 800,000 (and still counting) graves in Nécropolis Cristóbal Colón, the most famous cemetery in Latin America, one site receives far more flowers than any other. At the corner of Calles 1 and F, Cubans from all walks of life visit the raised white tomb of Amelia Goyri de la Hoz, the country's unofficial patron saint of lost causes. The story goes that this woman was buried with her infant son at her feet. When their bodies were exhumed, the mother was found clutching her baby to her chest. La Milagrosa, or the Miracle Woman, now attracts Cubans who ask for miracles. People who want to leave the country ask La Milagrosa for help to obtain their visas.

As the plethora
of flowers attest,
La Milagrosa still attracts
Cubans seeking miracles.

70. PLAZA DE LA REVOLUCIÓN

Between Avenida de Carlos Manuel de Céspedes and Avenida de la Independencia, south of Central Vedado

An enormous likeness of Che Guevara adorns the facade of the Ministry of the Interior on Plaza de la Revolución.

Fidel Castro had an office here in the Central Committee of the Communist Party building, formerly the Ministry of Justice headquarters. Although the monolithic architecture has a Soviet feel, most of the structures were built during Fulgencio Batista's regime. Whereas there were at least 10 newspapers in the nonintellectual Batista's day, the only influential literary source of information under Castro is the newspaper *Granma*, a Cuban *Pravda* published out of the Ministry of Interior office tower that displays the gigantic Che Guevara likeness in black. By comparison, technically clumsy and narrowly censored Cuban television at least has the redeeming characteristic of sometimes being laughable. The paranoid degree to which news and political thought is censored in Cuba makes intellectual freedom impossible.

71. COMANDANCIA DEL CHE

La Cabaña Fortress, east side of Bahía de La Habana

La Cabaña Fortress was built between 1763 and 1774 to protect Havana's harbour. After Fidel Castro took power, counterrevolutionaries were executed here during the "cleansing" trials chiefly overseen by Che Guevara. Guevara had witnessed the fall of liberal Jacobo Arbenz in Guatemala and had concluded that one of Arbenz's major mistakes while in power was not to eliminate reactionary elements. As well, Guevara had gained great respect from Castro and his fellow rebels when he volunteered to execute the rebels' first traitor in the Sierra Maestra. To kill was to be strong. Guevara's father was appalled by his son's bloodthirstiness when he visited Havana during the period of retribution, and never saw him again. First occupied on January 3, 1959, Che's command post is now preserved as a shrine.

72. CASTILLO DEL MORRO
East side of Bahía de La Habana

One of three forts built between 1558 and 1630 to protect Havana against pirates, Castillo de los Tres Santos Reyes Magnos del Morro, better known as El Morro, was successfully attacked by the British in July 1762, after which the British controlled Havana for 11 months and introduced much freer trade. More recently El Morro became infamous as a wretched prison for persecution of homosexuals. Reinaldo Arenas has described barbaric conditions in the dungeons of El Morro in his autobiography *Before Night Falls* (made into a movie in 2001). The dungeons hadn't been in use since the British victory. Some tolerance of homosexuality dawned tentatively in the 1990s, but the macho sensibilities of Fidel Castro and Che Guevara have mostly prevailed in Cuba since the revolution, often with a vengeance.

Since the 16th century, Castillo del Morro has guarded Havana against attackers.

73. CASA DE LAS AMÉRICAS
Calles 3 and G

Founded in 1959 to promote "sociocultural relations," the art deco Casa de las Américas is representative of Cuba's vigorous efforts to organize Latin and Caribbean countries to work together against American imperialism. While Cuba has played a direct role in the guerrilla movements in Nicaragua and Guatemala, it has also sponsored literary and artistic activities in the Americas. Unimpressive architecturally, this centre for international projects was directed by Haydée Santamaría, one of the two female

Haydée Santamaría, one of Fidel Castro's earliest supporters, was the director of Casa de las Américas for many years.

participants in Fidel Castro's attack on the Moncada Army Barracks. She committed suicide by shooting herself in the mouth with a .45 Colt pistol on July 26, 1980, the anniversary of the Moncada uprising. As one of two female participants in the Moncada Barracks assault, Santamaría lost both her brother, Abel, and her boyfriend in the botched attack. Although it's not widely discussed in Cuba, it is known that she became disillusioned with Castro prior to her suicide.

74. FEDERATION OF CUBAN WOMEN
Paseo No. 260, near Calle 13

This is the power centre for Vilma Espín, the Sierra Maestra rebel from an upper-class family who married, had children with, and eventually separated from Raúl Castro. Ostensibly a volunteer organization, the women's federation has long deducted 25 cents per month from the salaries of women who "choose" to join. Because accreditation is seen as a necessary criterion for promotion in Cuban society, it's rare to find a Cuban woman who isn't a member, whether she wants to be one or not. Espín's book *Cuban Women Confront the Future* looks at how women's lives have changed in Cuba after decades of Fidel Castro's regime.

Vilma Espín, who was with Fidel Castro in the Sierra Maestra in the 1950s, uses the Federation of Cuban Women as her power base.

75. HOTEL INGLATERRA
Paseo de Martí No. 416 at Calle San Rafael near Parque Central

Opened in 1856 and renovated in 1989, the oldest still-functioning hotel in Havana was the site of José Martí's 1879 speech in Havana advocating independence. Antonio Maceo stayed here in 1890. The Inglaterra staff is responsible for raising and lowering the Cuban flag for the white marble José Martí statue (said to be the oldest in Cuba) across the street. Because Hotel Inglaterra predates the Mafia hotels, its Louvre-like arcades seem dignified by comparison, but the Inglaterra is overpriced. The Spanish-operated Hostal Valencia, a converted mid-18th-century mansion near Plaza de Armas, provides 12 affordable rooms with high-ceilings and a great location.

This imposing statue of José
Martí looms opposite
Hotel Inglaterra.

76. CAPITOLIO NACIONAL
South of Parque Central

The seat of the Cuban Congress until 1959, this building now houses the Cuban Academy of Sciences and the National Library of Science and Technology. It was modelled directly on the Capitol building in Washington, D.C., and was erected in 1929 by 5,000 workers for $17 million as an initiative of President Gerardo Machado. Known as "The Butcher," Machado operated a terrorist regime that mainly protected U.S. business interests. He was toppled in 1933 by a general strike. At the centre of the

If the Capitolio Nacional looks overly familiar, it's because it's modelled after Washington, D.C.'s Capitol building.

Capitolio's 120-metre-long entrance hall is a replica of a 24-carat diamond that was placed in the floor to emphasize the "all roads lead to Rome" centrality of Havana. It was from this diamond, directly below the 62-metre-high dome, that all distances to Cuba's towns were to be measured. When President Grau Martín's World War II regime became too corrupt, he fled Cuba and took the diamond with him.

77. ZANELLI'S *CUBA*
Salón de los Pasos Pérdidos, Capitolio

Inside the Capitolio is reputedly the third-largest indoor statue in the world, eclipsed only by a statue of Buddha in Japan and the Lincoln Memorial in Washington. It's a 49-tonne, 17-metre statue of a golden female figure,

Angelo Zanelli's *Cuba* is said to be the third-largest indoor statue in the world.

representing the Cuban republic, by Italian sculptor Angelo Zanelli. The Capitolio contains two more 15-tonne, seven-metre statues by Zanelli, and a room that honours Simón Bolívar, the South American liberator. At the building's entrance are little-noticed busts of pre-Machado American puppet rulers José Miguel Gómez, Mario García Menocal, and Alfredo Zayas. After Machado came Ramón Grau San Martín (overthrown by Fulgencio Batista) and a series of Batista appointees as president, followed by the election of Carlos Prío Socarrás in 1948. When Prío was tossed from power, the people destroyed his statue but left behind his feet.

78. FOUNTAIN OF INDIA
Between Parque de la Fraternidad and Calle Máximo Gómez, north of the junction between Calle Dragones and Paseo de Martí

This "Noble Havana" statue honours a legendary Indian queen after whom Havana is said to be named. The original town site of "noble" Havana was on the southern coast of Cuba at Batabano, and was chosen in 1515 by one of Diego Velázquez's men, Pánfilo de Narváez. Plagued by mosquitoes, the first "Habaneros" moved to the mouth of the Río Chorrera, then moved down the coast to the present site where San Cristóbal de La Habana was founded. This is one of two famous statues by Giuseppe Gaginni, the other being the Fountain of Lions in the Plaza de San Francisco. Fetchingly clad in palm leaves and feathers, the "Indian" maiden holds a cornucopia and a shield bearing the arms of Havana.

79. HAVANA CHESS ACADEMY

Across from the Capitolio

Cuban world chess champion José Raúl Capablanca most often played chess here. In his heyday Capablanca was as exalted as any contemporary pop star. The Havana Chess Academy has long since been torn down and replaced by a sports centre for chess, weightlifting, judo, and handball. This new sports academy was built for the 1991 Pan-American Games, a collective triumph during which Cuba won 140 gold medals and the United States took 130.

World chess champion José Raúl Capablanca often played his game at the Havana Chess Academy.

80. GRAN TEATRO DE LA HABANA

Paseo de Martí No. 458 between Calles San Rafael and San Martín

The present 2,000-seat theatre and its adjoining recital and rehearsal halls are said to constitute the oldest functioning theatre in the Americas. This is based on connections to the adjoining Galician Centre (Galicia is in northern Spain, where Fidel Castro's father was born). The Galician Centre was previously the home of Teatro Tacón. Here Giuseppe

Dancers practise at the Gran Teatro de La Habana, home of Cuba's national ballet and opera companies.

Verdi operas were performed in 1846. Built at a cost of $2 million, with a central chandelier that held 1,000 lights, Teatro Tacón was named for pompish Governor Miguel Tacón and was constructed by a famous Havana criminal named Francisco Marty. These two men met when Marty complied with the governor's offer to become an informer against his fellow smugglers. After the local authorities conducted several successful raids, the governor offered ex-smuggler Marty his promised reward. But Marty asked instead for a monopoly on fish sales. He established a new fish market on one of Havana's two oldest streets, Empedrado, and became rich. Marty then struck a similar deal to erect Teatro Tacón. With great entrepreneurial skill

Marty ran the theatre for the city's avid opera-goers just as he controlled the fish market. This ex-smuggler and informer turned respectable impresario was loathed by his underpaid singers and thespians whose services he monopolized. Today the Gran Teatro is home to the national ballet and opera companies.

81. PALACIO DE LOS MATRIMONIOS

Paseo de Martí No. 302, one block south of Hotel Sevilla

On Saturdays many relaxed couples arrive in fancy cars at the Palace of Marriages to get hitched. Himself a bastard, Fidel Castro hasn't made the sanctity of marriage into a top priority. Whereas there was only one divorce for every 19 marriages in

A Cuban bride arrives for her wedding at the Palacio de los Matrimonios.

1953, almost 50 percent of marriages ended in divorce by 1990, many constrained by cramped living conditions. In 1989 some 61 percent of births were out of wedlock. The Roman Catholic Church doesn't stipulate morals in Cuba anymore, so few Cubans care that their leader has at least eight illegitimate children. Promiscuity wasn't a major problem until the tourists returned in large numbers. Now Castro has been forced to crack down on a wave of prostitution since the 1990s. Prostitutes in 18th-century Havana were once forbidden to solicit directly on the street, an edict that essentially returned in dollar-mad Havana at the dawn of the 21st century. Special police patrol the tourist areas, and *jineteras* ("jockeys") must be very careful to avoid jail detentions. Castro has kept his own sex life exceedingly private. Meanwhile Cuba has one of the most extreme programs to combat AIDS in the world: mandatory testing and mandatory quarantine if found to be HIV positive. During all this flux, the Palace of Marriages has replaced churches for weddings.

Seen here giving a radio address, dictator Fulgencio Batista was a frequent habitué of Hotel Sevilla.

82. HOTEL SEVILLA
Calle Trocadero No. 55 between Paseo de Martí and Calle Agramonte

In January 1955, U.S. Vice President Richard Nixon attended an extravagant rooftop party here with Fulgencio
Batista and his Mafia friends. Nixon likened Batista to
Abraham Lincoln. Known as the Pretty Mulatto, Batista
had risen from lowly circumstances in Oriente Province,
where Fidel Castro grew up, and had once worked for
Castro's father. With mixed Indian, Spanish, and black
blood, Batista was never fully accepted or respected by the
Cuban establishment that partied at the Havana Yacht Club
and what was then known as the Sevilla-Biltmore. The
lobby of the Sevilla contains a photo gallery of its most
famous guests such as the *New York Times'* Herbert Matthews.
The hotel was also featured in Graham Greene's novel *Our
Man in Havana*, a portrait of corruption.

83. LA CORONA
TOBACCO FACTORY
West of Pavillón Granma on Calle Refugio

Any historical tour of Cuba can't be complete without at
least some mention of the importance of the tobacco industry and cigars. Tobacco was grown commercially as early
as 1580 and became the top export in 1700. The finest tobacco is from Pinar del Río, Cuba's westernmost province,
where 80 percent of the tobacco crop is harvested. Cubans
say the best tobacco is grown either along the Río Cuyaguateje
or at Hoyo de Monterrey, both southwest of the city of
Pinar del Río in the Vuelta Abajo region. A converted prison,

A typical factory worker can roll 90 cigars per day.

the Ricardo Donatien Factory at Calle Maceo No. 157 in the city of Pinar del Río is typical of manufacturing plants throughout Cuba where approximately 80 workers can produce more than 12,000 cigars per day. An average roller manufactures 90 cigars per day. The Corona Factory was founded in 1842. Two of the other best-known cigar factories in Havana are Partagás near the Capitolio and Casa del Tabaco in Miramar. The top-quality tobacco goes to the Corona Factory as well as to the H. Upmann, Partagás, Romeo y Julieta, and El Laguito factories. Before Fidel Castro reluctantly gave up smoking cigars in the mid-1980s, he favoured the Cohiba brand.

84. MUSEO ABEL SANTAMARÍA
Calle 25 No. 164 between Calles Infanta and O

Here Abel and his sister, Haydée, lived and sometimes played host to a young Fidel Castro. If you traipse up the flight of stairs to the sixth floor, more often than not Santamaría's two-room suite won't be open for public viewing. It's a dingy, dark apartment block by North American and European standards, but not an atypical one by Cuban standards. Abel Santamaría is one of the best-known martyrs of the revolution. Many streets and parks in Cuba are named in his honour in keeping with Castro's strict direction that no parks, schools, streets, et cetera, can be named after a living person.

85. PAVILLÓN *GRANMA*

Between Avenida de las Misiones and Calles Colón, Agramonte, and Trocadero, near the Museo de la Revolución

The *Granma* brought Fidel Castro and his rebels back to Cuba in 1957 to start the revolution.

The actual voyage of the *Granma*, like the Moncada Army Barracks assault, was a disaster. One of the 82 men on the cramped yacht fell overboard, the boat arrived late, and it dropped the rebels off in a swamp, but this oddly named vessel (*Gramma* misspelled) has sailed into Cuban history with official importance as if it constitutes Castro's version of Noah's Ark. The yacht, bought by Castro from an American in Mexico, is so protected in a cage-like enclosure that a better impression of the *Granma* can only be gained if one flies to the other side of the country to Playa de las Coloradas, site of the landing, where there is an exact-size replica in an empty parking lot.

86. MUSEO DE LA REVOLUCIÓN

Calle Refugio No. I

Dedicated to Fidel Castro's regime and its revolutionary triumph, this former presidential palace is a museum that features ghoulish life-size replicas of Che Guevara and Camilo Cienfuegos, Fidel Castro's Soviet tank from the Bay of Pigs encounter, extensive memorabilia, a casket to commemorate Guevara, photos of Tania the Guerrilla, pictures of Guevara's undercover disguises, and a Cretins' Corner that ridicules the likes of Fulgencio Batista and Ronald Reagan. Batista's

As seen in this photograph, Che Guevara was a master of disguise.

office has been preserved, including his secret stairway for fast getaways.

87. UNIVERSIDAD DE LA HABANA

Calles Neptuno and San Lázaro

Founded in 1728, this was the only university in Cuba until 1963. It began as the Royal and Pontifical University of San Geronimo de La Habana and was secularized in 1842. The move to its present site commenced in 1905. Here Fidel Castro somehow managed to earn his law degree while mostly fomenting unrest and concentrating on his political ambitions and gang war during the 1950s. Cuban society accords the term *doctor* to its lawyers, consequently Castro likes to present himself as Dr. Fidel Castro, much to the irritation of his harshest critics. Here, as well, Castro first met the beautiful socialite Naty Revuelta, who would give him an estranged daughter, Alina Fernández. Castro was an indifferent student, but he has always been an avid reader. He says his favourite book is Miguel de Cervantes's *Don Quixote*, a story about an obsessive, deranged idealist.

88. MONUMENTO A JULIO ANTONIO MELLA

Across from the entrance to Universidad de La Habana

Founder of the Cuban Communist Party (CCP), Julio Antonio Mella was assassinated by the Gerardo Machado regime while in Mexico in 1929. His lover at the time was artist Tina Modotti, a contemporary of Diego Rivera and Frida Kahlo. This modest monument recognizes Mella and the importance of the Communist Party. By the eve of the Soviet Union's collapse, approximately

This bust of Julio Antonio Mella honours the assassinated founder of the Cuban Communist Party.

84 percent of Cuba's trade was with Communist countries. By October 1991 the CCP had adopted a resolution for profit-maximizing state-owned corporations that operate independently of government. Foreign investors can repatriate profits, and there are introductory exemptions for taxes. A far cry from Mella's Marxism.

The Obelisco de Marianao, dedicated to the doctor who helped defeat yellow fever, is shaped like an injection needle.

89. BLACK VOMIT

Carlos J. Finlay Exhibit, Museo de la Historia Natural, at Calles Cuba and Lamparilla

The Museo de la Historia Natural, the oldest museum in Cuba, was established in 1874. It hosted Albert Einstein's last public address in 1930 and showcases the pharmacy and research office of the medical scientist Carlos J. Finlay (1833–1915), who discovered the agent that transmits yellow fever, a scourge known in colonial Cuba as the Black Vomit. Born in Camagüey, Finlay discovered in 1881 that a certain type of mosquito was the carrier of the disease. The second U.S. governor of Cuba, General Leonard Wood, himself a doctor, conducted a successful campaign to eradicate yellow fever from Cuba in the early 1900s. There is also a modest Finlay memorial at the intersections of Calles 41, 47, and 49, and a more prominent Obelisco de Marianao at Calle 114 and Avenida 41. The obelisk is strangely but appropriately shaped like an injection needle.

90. HOTEL HABANA LIBRE

Calle L between Calles 23 and 25

It's not mentioned in the guidebooks, but if you persistently and politely inquire at the desk of Havana's largest hotel, you can sometimes arrange to visit the 22nd-floor room that served as Fidel Castro's living quarters and office when he first attained power in 1959. Here one can imagine the bizarre tryst between the bearded Fidel and his live-in American girlfriend Marita Lorenz. All the leading figures of Castro's revolution ran the country from the 22nd floor in 1959 when it was still the Havana Hilton. The gang included Celia Sánchez, Che Guevara, Camilo Cienfuegos, and Raúl Castro. Many tourists stay here and don't realize the hotel's place in Cuba's history.

One of Havana's ubiquitous coco-taxis waits outside Hotel Capri, the onetime haunt of gangsters Meyer Lansky and Santo Trafficante, Jr.

91. HOTEL CAPRI
Calle 21 No. 8 at Calle N

Meyer Lansky's main collaborator in the expansion of gambling and casinos was Florida mobster Santo Trafficante, Jr., who helped manage the Hotels Capri, Sevilla-Biltmore, Commodoro, Deauville, and Riviera. The tough-guy emcee at the Capri's Red Room was American actor George Raft, famous for his portrayals of gangsters in Hollywood movies. A 1994 autobiography by Frank Ragano, *Mob Lawyer*, repeats the story that when Massachusetts Senator John F. Kennedy was a guest of Trafficante at his Hotel Commodoro, Trafficante and his casino partner, Everisto García, hired three prostitutes for the future president. The foursome was secretly filmed in the young senator's bedroom. Trafficante later became the Mafia figure most closely associated with Lee Harvey Oswald's assassination of Kennedy in Dallas. The mobster was also an acquaintance of Jack Ruby. There's a photo of Trafficante in Hotel Sevilla's lobby.

92. HOTEL NACIONAL
Calles 21 and O

In December 1946 Frank Sinatra was hired to sing for America's top gangsters at a Mafia summit here to welcome Charles "Lucky" Luciano back to the fold. Luciano, the Boss of Bosses, had been deported from the United States and had been living in Rome. With a false passport he had rejoined his old cohort Meyer Lansky in Havana in October. Lansky and Luciano met on December 22 with *mafiosi* Frank Costello, Tommy Lucchese, Vito Genovese,

Here you can imagine Frank Sinatra crooning to the notorious *mafioso* Charles "Lucky" Luciano at the palatial Hotel Nacional.

Moe Dalitz, Joe "Bananas" Bonanno, Joe Adonis, Albert Anastasia, Tony Accardo, Carlo Marcello, "Dandy" Phil Kastel, and Santo Trafficante, Jr. At the time Luciano was hoping to transform the Isla de Pinos (renamed Isla de la Juventud in 1978) into a gambling Mecca to rival Monte Carlo. U.S. federal narcotics agents tracked down Luciano, and he was forced to return to Italy, leaving Lansky in control of their shared plans. Hotel Nacional, in the suburb of Vedado, was originally modelled in the 1920s on the Breakers Hotel in Palm Beach.

93. HOTEL RIVIERA
Paseo and Malecón

Opened in 1957, the Riviera was home to Meyer Lansky who lived in a 20th-floor suite. Reputedly once in competition with John F. Kennedy's father, Joseph, in the bootlegging business, Lansky was the kingpin of American *mafiosi* who helped to install Fulgencio Batista as Cuba's president. On March 10, 1952, Batista staged a coup, suspended the Constitution, cancelled elections, and became dictator. The Truman administration in Washington, D.C., approved and sent aid. Thanks to payoffs to Batista, Mafia hotel revenues were tax-free. Lansky and Batista both fled Cuba on January 1, 1959.

Florida's Santo Trafficante, Jr., who ran Hotel Riviera, is the mobster most closely linked to the assassination of President John F. Kennedy.

94. MONUMENTO A LAS VÍCTIMAS DEL *MAINE*

Malecón, near Hotel Nacional

Two rusting cannons honour the 266 American sailors who died after an 1898 explosion in Havana's harbour aboard the USS *Maine*. American officers were conspicuously absent onshore during the tragedy. The explosion was used by American newspapers to foment anti-Spanish sentiment. Fidel Castro's regime has added a plaque that states: "To the victims of the *Maine*, who were sacrificed by imperialist voracity in its eagerness to seize the island of Cuba." At the junction of Paseo and Calle Zapata, Castro's government has also erected a modest plaque for Julius and Ethel Rosenberg, the American couple who were executed in 1953 for passing secrets to the Soviet Union. The inscription reads: "Murdered June 19, 1953," with Julius Rosenberg's words "For peace, bread, and roses, we face the executioners." Other perceived victims of American imperialism are also

This monument recalls the mysterious explosion that killed 266 American sailors aboard the *Maine* in 1898.

commemorated in Havana. There's a beach named after Congo nationalist Patrice Lumumba, and a sports stadium named after Chilean nationalist Salvadore Allende, leaders who were murdered by the CIA.

95. MALECÓN

The Muro del Malecón, the famous perimeter wall and walkway around Habana Vieja, was begun in 1901 from La Punta in order to drain and protect Havana's urban centre. After another 50 years, the construction reached the mouth of the Río Almendares, seven kilometres from La Punta. Pummelled by waves, the Malecón has long been a Mecca for lovers and prostitutes. "The long wall becomes a long line of endless kisses," according to one official tourist guide. At night, beware.

Havana's Malecón has been the city's quintessential people place ever since Fidel Castro's rebels marched along the broad seaside avenue at the outset of 1960.

96. UNION OF WRITERS AND ARTISTS OF CUBA

Calle 17 between Calles G and H, Vedado District

Poet Nicolás Guillén *(left)* served as the president of the Union of Writers and Artists of Cuba for many years.

Countless writers and artists have been persecuted, intimidated, humiliated, imprisoned, or expelled from Cuba since Fidel Castro gained power. Here, until his death in 1989, the national poet Nicolás Guillén did the bidding of Castro for many years as the writers' and artists' union president. In 1962 Castro succinctly defined the parameters for artists and intellectuals in Cuba: "Within the revolution, everything; outside the revolution, nothing."

97. CELIA SÁNCHEZ'S FIRST HAVANA RESIDENCE
Calle 11 No. 1007, Vedado District

Where Fidel Castro sleeps, and who might sleep with him, are facts not for publication. But we know from reading *New York Times* correspondent Herbert Matthews's underappreciated 1961 memoir *The Cuban Story*, in which he describes his friendship and subsequent criticisms of Castro at length, that Castro mainly slept at Celia Sánchez's "shabby" apartment in the early 1960s. Matthews spent Castro's 34th birthday with him, first meeting El Jefe at this address. "Most nights he is in Celia's apartment. She is a brave, simple, gentle, pious creature." This modest apartment was furnished from the Sánchez house in Pilón.

98. RUSSIAN EMBASSY
Avenida 5 at Calle 65, Miramar District

The freakishly forlorn Russian Embassy, where Fidel was known as Fido, now stands out like an architectural sore thumb. Not far from here, on Avenida 1, is the dilapidated Teatro Karl Marx (formerly Teatro Blanquita), which has also fallen into disrepair. Economically Cuba wasn't able to rebound from the withdrawal of Soviet aid as of 1989. With the loss of nearly $8 billion per year, the country was

The Russian Embassy
has fallen on hard times
since the withdrawal
of Soviet aid.

forced to implement severe rationing. As well, millions of Cubans stuck with Soviet cars and dingy Soviet apartments learned the hard way that Soviet technology can seem like a contradiction in terms. The Russians aren't missed.

99. CANADIAN EMBASSY
Calle 30 No. 518, near Avenida 7, Miramar District

The two Western countries that have consistently refused to buckle to American pressure in terms of their relations with Cuba are the United States' closest neighbours, Canada and Mexico. They are the only two nations in the Western Hemisphere that maintained relations with Cuba after the United States purged Cuba from the Organization of American States. Prior to the invasion of Cuba by Castro on the *Granma*, Mexico provided an uneasy haven for the revolutionaries. Since then Canada has led the way in encouraging business investment and tourism. In 1992, after President George Bush Senior signed a bill now called the Torricelli Act—an extraterritorial ruling to forbid subsidiaries of American companies from trading with Cuba and to forbid ships from docking at American ports within six months of their docking in Cuba—the Canadian ambassador to Cuba, Madame Lorangel, openly criticized

The Canadian Embassy in Havana once played host to Prime Minister Pierre Elliott Trudeau and his wife, Margaret, when they made a state visit to Cuba in 1976.

the American embargo. Canada has remained opposed to the Helms-Burton Act, a tightening of the American embargo on Cuba. There is a U.S. Interest Office in the Swiss Embassy at Avenida 5 No. 2005, but diplomatic relations have remained tense. President Bill Clinton's administration failed to make significant changes to the status quo. Cuba's special relationship with Canada was triggered by a 1976 state visit by Prime Minister Pierre Elliott Trudeau, his wife, Margaret, and their infant son, Michel. Both Trudeau and Castro were taught by the same Jesuit, Father Jean Chadwick, who had Trudeau as a student at the Collège Jean-de-Brébeuf in Montreal and Castro as a student at Colegio Belén in Havana.

100. TROPICANA NIGHTCLUB
Calle 72 No. 4504 at Avenida 43, Marianao District

Cuba's most famous nightclub opened in 1939. The scantily clad dancing girls over the years have shared the stage with the likes of Maurice Chevalier and Nat King Cole. A garden fountain of nubile nymphs tries to create the impression that Cuba is a playground, but "paradise under the stars" in socialist Cuba is still reserved for the rich. Not far away in Miramar, adventurous travellers can find one of the country's top venues for music, Casa de La Musica, at Calle 20 and Avenida 35. The Tropicana is all very well if you have money to burn, and there's an equivalent Tropicana cabaret in Santiago de Cuba, but just as many tourists might like to visit the Buena Vista Social Club—if it still existed in the nearby Buena Vista neighbourhood. The subject of that popular documentary film of the same name, made by American Ry Cooder, was torn down long ago.

The Fountain of Nymphs outside the famed Tropicana Nightclub tries hard to dispel the stern image of socialist Cuba.

101. COJÍMAR

Fishing village, 10 kilometres east of Havana

Ernest Hemingway kept his boat *Pilar* in Cojímar when he wasn't fishing or patrolling for Nazi submarines. There is a bust of Hemingway next to El Torreón fort, north of La Terraza Restaurant, immortalized in *The Old Man and the Sea*. Gregorio Fuentes, Hemingway's fishing companion, cook, and *Pilar* captain since the late 1930s, was often alleged to be the model for the main character in Hemingway's Nobel Prize–winning novel. In fact, Hemingway and Fuentes once came across an old man in the Florida Straits trying to land a huge marlin. Seeing the old-timer struggle with his catch, they offered to help. Their offer was declined. Hemingway later learned the old man died in his efforts to land the marlin. That inspired the book. Born in the Canary Islands in 1897, Fuentes came to live in

Cojímar at age six and never left. He spent two years with Hemingway during World War II, roaming the waters around Cuba, a Thompson machine gun bolted to the gunwale of the *Pilar*. After spending two decades in Cuba, Hemingway gave the *Pilar* to Fuentes. The former fish merchant and at-sea bartender supposedly "donated" the boat to the Cuban government shortly after Hemingway committed suicide in Idaho in 1961. Fuentes was a tourist magnet at La Terraza until his death at age 104 in 2002.

Ernest Hemingway's beloved *Pilar*, once birthed in Cojímar, is now on permanent display at Finca la Vigía, his former home.

SOURCES

Aeberhard, Danny, ed. *Cuba*. 3rd ed. Hong Kong: Insight Guides, APA Publications, 2002.

Anderson, Jon Lee. *Che Guevara: A Revolutionary Life*. New York: Grove Press, 1997.

Arenas, Reinaldo. *Before Night Falls: A Memoir*. New York: Viking Penguin, 1993.

Baker, Christopher P. *Cuba Handbook*. Chico, CA: Moon Publications, 1997.

Barclay, Juliet. *Havana: Portrait of a City*. London: Cassell, 1993.

Benítez-Rojo, Antonio. *The Repeating Island: The Caribbean and the Postmodern Perspective*. Translated by James Maraniss. Durham, NC: Duke University Press, 1992.

Betto, Frei. *Fidel & Religion*. Melbourne: Ocean Press, 1990.

Bourne, Peter G. *Fidel: A Biography of Fidel Castro*. New York: Dodd, Mead, 1986.

Brân, Zoë. *Enduring Cuba*. Footscray, Australia: Lonely Planet, 2002.

Cabrera Infante, Guillermo. *Mea Cuba*. New York: Farrar, Straus & Giroux, 1994.

Castro, Fidel. *History Will Absolve Me*. Havana: Ediciones Politicas, Editorial de Ciencias Sociales, Cuban Book Institute, 1975.

CIA Targets Fidel: Secret 1967 CIA Inspector General's Report on Plots to Assassinate Fidel Castro. Melbourne: Ocean Press, 1996.

Coe, Andrew. *Cuba*. 2nd ed. Lincolnwood, IL: NTC Publishing Group, Passport Books, 1997.

Collier, Peter, and David Horowitz. *The Kennedys: An American Drama*. New York: Summit Books, 1984.

Crankshaw, Edward. *Khrushchev: A Career*. New York: Viking Press, 1966.

Debray, Régis. *Prison Writings*. London: Penguin Books, 1975.

Face to Face with Fidel Castro: A Conversation with Tomás Borge. Melbourne: Ocean Press, 1993.

Fernández, Alina. *Castro's Daughter: An Exile's Memoir of Cuba*. New York: St. Martin's Press, 1998.

Franklin, Jane. *Cuba and the United States: A Chronological History*. Melbourne: Ocean Press, 1997.

Furiati, Claudia. *ZR Rifle: The Plot to Kill Kennedy and Castro*. Melbourne: Ocean Press, 1994.

Geyer, Georgie Anne. *Guerrilla Prince: The Untold Story of Fidel Castro*. Boston: Little, Brown, 1991.

Gimbel, Wendy. *Havana Dreams: A Story of Cuba*. New York: Vintage Random House, 1998.

Gorry, Conner. *Cuba*. 3rd ed. Footscray, Australia: Lonely Planet, 2004.

Guevara, Che. *Che Guevara Speaks: Selected Speeches and Writings*. Edited by G. Lavan. Zim Pan African Publishers Ltd. and José Martí Publishing House, 1988.

Halperin, Maurice. *The Taming of Fidel Castro*. Berkeley: University of California Press, 1979.

Hartmann Matos, Alejandro. *Les Français à Baracoa*. Valencia, 1999.

_____. *Los Días de Colón en Baracoa*. Valencia, 1995.

Holt-Seeland, Inger. *Women of Cuba*. Westport, CT: Lawrence Hill & Co. Inc., 1982.

Hungry Wolf, Adolf. *Letters from Cuba*. Skookumchuck, BC: Canadian Caboose Press, 1996.

_____. *Trains of Cuba*. Skookumchuck, BC: Canadian Caboose Press, 1996.

Iyer, Pico. *Cuba and the Night*. New York: Knopf, 1995.

Lewis, Oscar, and Ruth M. Lewis and Susan M. Rigdon. *Living the Revolution: An Oral History of Contemporary Cuba*. Urbana: University of Illinois Press, 1977.

Lorenz, Marita, and Ted Schwarz. *Marta: One Woman's Extraordinary Tale of Love and Espionage from Castro to Kennedy*. New York: Thunder's Mouth Press, 1993.

Moore, Marjorie, and Adrienne Hunter. *Seven Women and the Cuban Revolution*. Toronto: Lugus Publications, 1997.

Pendle, George. *A History of Latin America*. Baltimore: Penguin, 1963.

Pérez, Louis A., Jr. *The War of 1898: The United States and Cuba in History and Historiography*. Chapel Hill: University of North Carolina Press, 1998.

Ponce de León, Juana, and Esteban Ríos Rivera, eds. *Dream with No Name: Contemporary Fiction from Cuba*. New York: Seven Stories Press, 1999.

Reporting on Cuba. Ensayo Book Institute Havana, 1967.

Ripley, C. Peter. *Conversations with Cuba*. Athens: University of Georgia Press, 1999.

Ryan, Alan, ed. *The Reader's Companion to Cuba*. San Diego: Harcourt Brace & Company, 1997.

Simons, G. L. *Cuba: From Conquistador to Castro*. New York: St. Martin's Press, 1996.

Soldevila, Carlos. *Cuba*. 2nd ed. Montreal: Ulysses Travel Publications, 1999.

Szulc, Tad. *Fidel: A Critical Portrait*. New York: William Morrow, 1986.

Thomas, Hugh. *Cuba: The Pursuit of Freedom*. New York: Harper & Row, 1971.

Ward, Fred. *Inside Cuba Today*. New York: Crown Publishers, 1978.

Williams, Diana. *Diving and Snorkeling Guide to Cuba*. Houston, TX: Pisces Books, 1996.

Willinsky, John. *Learning to Divide the World: Education at Empire's End*. Minneapolis: University of Minnesota Press, 1998.

Yebra García, Rita María. *All Havana*. Com-Relieve, S.A. y Editorial Escudo de Oro, S.A., fourth edition, undated.

In addition to the above publications, the author has consulted many periodicals, chiefly *The Guardian Weekly*, *The New Yorker*, *Granma* (English editions), and *Amnesty International* reports.